Oxford International Primary

W0036214

4

Science

Workbook

Deborah Roberts
Terry Hudson

Alan Haigh
Geraldine Shaw

Language consultants:
John McMahon
Liz McMahon

OXFORD

Great Clarendon Street, Oxford, OX2 6DP, United Kingdom

Oxford University Press is a department of the University of Oxford. It furthers the University's objective of excellence in research, scholarship, and education by publishing worldwide. Oxford is a registered trade mark of Oxford University Press in the UK and in certain other countries.

British Library Cataloguing in Publication Data

Data available

ISBN 978-1-382006637

9 10 8

Paper used in the production of this book is a natural, recyclable product made from wood grown in sustainable forests. The manufacturing process conforms to the environmental regulations of the country of origin.

Printed in China by Golden Cup

Acknowledgements

The publisher and authors would like to thank the following for permission to use photographs and other copyright material:

Cover: Artwork by Blindsalida. Photos: **p19(l):** Madlen/Shutterstock; **p19(m):** Roxana Bashyrova/Shutterstock; **p19(r):** koosen/Shutterstock; **p39(a):** Iakov Filimonov/Shutterstock/DAM; **p39(b):** Pu Su Lan/Shutterstock; **p39(c):** Corbis; **p39(d):** Digital Stock/Corbis; **p39(e):** Digital Stock/Corbis; **p44:** Zuzana Randlova/Dreamstime; **p48(a):** Anne Kitzman/Shutterstock; **p48(b):** Weerachai chandang/Shutterstock; **p48(c):** Joseph Sohm/Shutterstock; **p48(d):** Sonia Bonet/Shutterstock; **p48(e):** Sonia Bonet/Shutterstock; **p50:** Nature Picture Library/Alamy Stock Photo; **p54(a):** DoublePHOTO studio/Shutterstock; **p54(b):** Vibrant Image Studio/Shutterstock; **p54(c):** JRP Studio/Shutterstock; **p54(d):** Sky Light Pictures/Shutterstock; **p54(e):** Olha Rohulya/Shutterstock; **p61:** Cool Vector Maker/Shutterstock; **p85:** Quincy Russell, Mona Lisa Production/Science Photo Library; **p91(l):** Richard Codington/Alamy Stock Photo; **p91(r):** Jim Cumming/Alamy Stock Photo; **p109:** Chaichan Ingkawaranon/Alamy Stock Photo; **p128:** Monty Rakusen/Cultura/Getty Images; **p134:** Lourens Smak/Alamy Stock Photo.

Artwork by Q2A Media Services Pvt. Ltd.

Every effort has been made to contact copyright holders of material reproduced in this book. Any omissions will be rectified in subsequent printings if notice is given to the publisher.

Contents

How to Use this Book

The Workbook for *Oxford International Primary Science* supports the Student Book that children are using in their science lessons for this year.

The Student Book includes some pair, group and whole-class activities, hands-on tasks and write-in tasks to test students' understanding and help them learn. It is important to extend these tasks. This Workbook enables students to build on what they have learned in the Student Book to develop a secure understanding of scientific concepts.

Encouraging students to think about and apply their growing skills and knowledge helps them consolidate their understanding and work scientifically. This helps with confidence. Students also have opportunities to see that science is relevant all around them – both inside and outside the classroom.

Students may find it useful to complete an investigation planning form. This sets out all the stages of the investigation. A proforma is provided in the Teacher's Guide. Find out more at:

http://www.oxfordprimary.com/international-science

Structure of the book

This Workbook is divided into five units plus a Support for Teachers and Parents section and a Quiz:

Support for Teachers and Parents
Unit 1 Solids, Liquids and Gases
Unit 2 Habitats
Unit 3 Digestion and Food Chains
Unit 4 Electricity
Unit 5 Sounds
Quiz Yourself

What you will find in each unit

There are four types of lessons:

Key words and introduction lessons encourage students to read, spell and use the scientific vocabulary in the unit.

Activities build on the work in the Student Book. These help with developing language skills, developing scientific enquiry skills, applying mathematical knowledge and securing understanding rather than just recall. The Support for Teachers and Parents notes on pages 6–13 give you advice on how to help students with each activity.

What have I learned encourages students to talk about what they have learned, reflect on what went well and revisit any areas they need to check. This encourages a growth mindset.

Investigate like a scientist enables students to apply what they have learned in practical contexts.

What you will find in the lessons

Icons show the nature of each task:

Discuss: Students are encouraged to discuss and communicate scientific ideas and approaches. They can work in pairs or small groups for discussion tasks.

Investigate: Students are encouraged to plan, ask questions and record results for each investigation. They are asked to observe closely, make predictions and compare their results with others. Sometimes you will use different equipment, which is available in school. You may also ask students to carry out a test in a different way, to make sure they are safe.

Language support: This icon highlights activities that provide language support through writing frames or word banks. Students are encouraged to write, read and record short answers.

Hints and tips: Students are encouraged to think about tips to make investigations safer or more effective.

Stretch zone: Students are encouraged to extend their understanding.

Mindful moments: Students are encouraged to think about and reflect on what they have learned. This supports students' well-being.

What went well: Students are encouraged to talk about what went well in each module to secure their understanding.

Student Book

Throughout the Workbook, you will find links to the Student Book. Students can refer to information in the Student Book to help them complete activities.

Teacher's Guide

The Teacher's Guide that accompanies this book provides lesson notes and answers for each page.

Support for Teachers and Parents

1 Solids, Liquids and Gases

What students will learn

This unit helps students to understand more about solids, liquids and gases. They will identify a range of solids, liquids and gases and explore how materials change between these states due to temperature changes. Students will also learn about the roles of evaporation and condensation in the water cycle and investigate the link between the rate of evaporation and temperature. Students will:

- compare and group materials together, according to whether they are solids, liquids or gases
- observe that some materials change state when they are heated or cooled, and measure or research the temperature at which this happens in degrees Celsius (°C)
- identify the part played by evaporation and condensation in the water cycle and associate the rate of evaporation with temperature.

> **Key words**
> condensation, evaporation, freezing, gas, liquid, melting, solid, temperature, water cycle

Scientific enquiry skills

This unit helps students to develop and practise the following scientific enquiry skills.

Scientific enquiry skill	Page
Ask questions	20, 22, 25, 28, 37
Use equipment	20, 21, 22, 23, 24, 25, 26, 27, 28, 31, 33, 37
Observe	14, 15, 17, 18, 21, 22, 23, 24, 25, 26, 27, 28, 30, 31, 33, 37
Measure	20, 22, 25, 28
Compare	16, 17, 18, 20, 22, 24, 25, 28, 30, 31
Notice patterns	16, 17, 22, 24, 25
Record	15, 16, 17, 18, 20, 22, 24, 25, 28, 30, 35, 37
Carry out tests	20, 21, 22, 24, 25, 28, 31, 33
Group/classify	17, 18, 24, 30
Use secondary sources	26, 27, 32, 34
Communicate findings	25, 29, 31, 32

Ways to help

- Encourage students to use the key words when they refer to the states of matter.
- Display a range of solids and liquids in the room so students can observe them.
- Ask students questions about the solids, liquids and gases they use every day.
- Ask students to think about why it is important that not all materials are solid.
- Encourage students to reflect on when they have seen ice being formed or melting.

Helping with activities

The following guidance gives you advice on how to help students with each activity.

What are solids, liquids and gases like?

Explain that the table is based on the one in the Student Book so students could look back at this if they have problems.

Identifying solids, liquids and gases

Have some examples available for students to look at and handle.

Examples of different states

Stress that students can draw all of the particles the same – only the space between the particles changes with solids, liquids and gases.

How are the particles arranged?

Tap a solid such as wood and pass your hand through the air to show that solids have closely packed particles and gases have particles that are far apart.

Investigate different shaped containers

Encourage students to measure the volume of the water carefully each time and to make sure all of the water is poured from the containers into the measuring jug.

Making a lava lamp

Point out that, although water and oil are both liquids, they behave differently and they do not mix.

Does air have weight?

Allow students to carry out the investigation a number of times, as it addresses a key misconception and shows that air does have weight.

Adding more particles

Ensure that the straw is sealed into the bag, so an airtight seal allows the bag to be inflated.

Investigate melting

Have some hot water available in a heatproof bowl and remind students not to touch the water.

Why salt the paths and roads?
Remind students to check their water in the freezer regularly. After time, even the water with the salt will freeze.

Evaporating and boiling
Explain that students can use words they have already learned in the unit. Point out the word box.

Particles and changes of state
Allow students to look back at their Student Book and earlier Workbook tasks if they need support in filling in the particle diagrams.

Keep ice cubes cool
Explain that this activity helps students to plan and carry out their investigation. Stress that they should fill in each section.

The damaged notebook
Point out the word box. Remind students to use these words to fill in the gaps.

Melting and freezing at home
Ask students to think about any examples of changes of state they have seen at home. Give a hint: remind them of ice cubes in drinks.

Ice displays
Have a collection of small models, toys and other objects that fit into a yoghurt carton.

Problems with steam
Once students have selected their topic, allow them access to research it to bring information to share with the group.

Using evaporation and condensation
Select a very sunny place for the solar stills. Remind students not to drink any of the water they collect.

Changes of state and the weather
Encourage students to look back at the water cycle in the Student Book if they need extra support.

Summary of changes of state
Point out the word box. It lists all words students need for the activities.

2 Habitats

What students will learn
This unit helps students to understand more about animals and plants and to explore how they are adapted to their habitats. They will study how identification keys can be used to name specific animals and plants. Students will also consider how humans can change habitats and endanger living things. Students will:

- observe and group living things
- investigate how different animals and plants live in different habitats
- learn how animals and plants are adapted to their habitats
- learn how to use identification keys to identify living things
- find out how human activity can change the environment and how this can put living things in danger.

> ### Key words
> environment, habitat, flowering plant, identification key, invertebrate, natural disaster, non-flowering plant, pollution, vertebrate

Scientific enquiry skills
This unit helps students to develop and practise the following scientific enquiry skills.

Scientific enquiry skill	Page
Ask questions	40, 41, 44, 46, 49, 50, 52, 53, 57
Use equipment	40, 41, 42, 43, 47, 48, 50, 52, 53, 56, 57, 60, 61
Observe	40, 41, 42, 43, 44, 47, 48, 50, 52, 53, 54, 56, 57, 60, 61
Measure	41, 44, 50, 52, 53, 60
Compare	39, 41, 44, 46, 47, 48, 50, 52, 53, 54, 55, 56, 57, 60
Notice patterns	39, 41, 42, 46, 48, 52, 53
Record	39, 40, 41, 44, 47, 48, 50, 52, 53, 54, 55, 60, 61
Carry out tests	40, 41, 44, 50, 52, 53, 55, 56, 57, 60, 61
Group/classify	40, 41, 46, 47, 48, 52, 53, 55
Use secondary sources	39, 42, 45, 47, 48, 49, 51, 57, 59
Communicate findings	40, 41, 42, 43, 45, 47, 50, 51, 52, 57, 59, 61

Ways to help

- Encourage students to highlight or underline key words when they write them.
- Download and print out photographs of living things to display in the room.
- Ask students questions about the animals and plants they see locally.

- Ask students to think about why living things need to be adapted to their habitats.
- Encourage students to think about adaptations by placing pictures of living things in unusual places – such as a polar bear on a coral reef.
- Display examples of identification keys and have a small library of identification books.
- Make a scrapbook of examples of earthquakes and volcanoes and use online films to show examples.

Helping with activities

The following guidance gives you advice on how to help students with each activity.

Mini-quadrats
Explain that a quadrat is a way of sampling at random to make a survey a fair test.

Investigate a habitat in the local environment
Identify some local habitats where students will see a range of plants and animals. Set up a part of the school grounds if possible by letting grass grow longer.

Making sense of data
Encourage students to place the dependent variable (what is being measured in an investigation) up the y-axis of a graph or chart. The animals go along the bottom (x-axis) and the numbers go up the side (y-axis) in this case.

Design your own animal
Show students some examples of animals adapted to cold climates to give them some clues about fat layers and body coverings.

Keeping cool
Ask students to think about where they would sit around the school or home to keep cool. Give hints about shade and breezes.

Adaptations to the environment
Have examples of photographs of local animals on the wall. Take students out to observe some in the wild.

Design a key
Point out that the type of key that students are designing only works with questions that have only two possible answers – e.g. 'yes' or 'no', or 'six legs' or 'eight legs'.

Survey of vertebrates
Take students to a variety of areas to see a range of vertebrates, such as woodlands, parks, ponds, the coastline or even a zoo.

Choosing a cactus for a friend
Allow students to have access to the internet or guidebooks about plants so they can research the cacti.

Florist survey
Invite a local florist, gardener or farmer in to talk about plants and how they identify them.

Cleaning up an oil spill
Remind students that oil will float on water. They should use this fact when planning their investigation.

Researching oil spills
Show films of examples of oil spills from online sources such as YouTube. Give students internet access so they can research their own examples.

Making an air pollution detector
Explain that only heavy particles in the air will settle and be trapped by their detectors. Other forms of pollution will not be measured.

Surface pollution survey
Point out that the sticky tape detector is actually used by scientists to measure surface pollution, but they will examine it using a microscope.

What impact do activities have on rivers?
Encourage students to discuss each of the photographs and think about how each impacts on rivers and the habitats.

Water survey
Talk students through the 1–5 scoring system for the level of pollution they will see.

Making waves
Demonstrate how to move the small piece of wood up and down to make small and large waves.

Protecting coastlines from tsunamis
Display examples of mangrove swamps – such as in the Caribbean, Kenya, South America and many countries in Asia such as Indonesia, Malaysia and Bangladesh – to show how closely packed the trees are.

Ash from volcanoes
Allow students to look back at their Student Book if they need support in labelling the volcano.

Advantages and disadvantages of volcanoes
Read through the advantages and disadvantages of volcanoes with students. Ask if any have seen any examples of these.

Earthquake-proof buildings
Pass around a 100-gram object so students can feel how strong their building must be. Hint that a wide base will be more stable than a narrow one.

Earthquake safety
Encourage students to imagine what people would do and feel if an earthquake happened.

3 Digestion and Food Chains

What students will learn

This unit helps students to understand how food is consumed and broken down to provide energy and nutrients to help humans live. Students will study the digestive system, including teeth and taste. They will also consider how feeding relationships can be represented by food chains and food webs. Students will:

- explore the digestive system in humans
- identify types of teeth and their functions
- explore the sense of taste
- find out how food chains can be used to show feeding relationships
- learn about the words 'producer', 'consumer', 'predator' and 'prey'
- explore and construct food chains for different habitats.

Key words
carnivore, consumer, digestive system, food chain, herbivore, omnivore, predator, prey, producer, taste, teeth

Scientific enquiry skills

This unit helps students to develop and practise the following scientific enquiry skills.

Scientific enquiry skill	Page
Ask questions	71, 72, 73, 76, 78, 84, 93
Use equipment	66, 69, 71, 72, 74, 79, 80, 81, 93
Observe	65, 69, 71, 72, 74, 78, 79, 80, 81, 82, 83, 85, 87, 90, 91, 93
Measure	76, 79, 86, 93
Compare	65, 66, 70, 71, 72, 73, 74, 75, 76, 78, 79, 80, 85, 91, 93
Notice patterns	66, 70, 71, 78, 79, 85, 87, 93
Record	66, 67, 68, 71, 72, 73, 76, 79, 81, 84, 86, 87, 89, 93
Carry out tests	69, 71, 72, 73, 74, 76, 79, 93
Group/classify	70, 71, 72, 75, 79, 90, 93
Use secondary sources	66, 68, 77, 81, 82, 90
Communicate findings	69, 71, 72, 73, 77, 79, 80, 81, 82, 84, 90

Ways to help

- Encourage students to use the key words for the digestive system when they talk about digestion.
- Download pictures of different food groups. Display them around the room.
- Obtain models of teeth and skulls to show the various types.
- Ask students to think about what they eat and why they need to eat it.
- Download pictures of plants and animals so that students can arrange them into different food chains.
- Make cards with producer, consumer, predator and prey. Students can add these to their food chains and food webs.

Helping with activities

The following guidance gives you advice on how to help students with each activity.

Energy in food
Remind students that the energy change can be calculated by subtracting the initial temperature from the final temperature.

Label the digestive system
Encourage students to look back at the picture and notes in their Student Book if they need support.

More about absorption
Remind students that if the surface area of the small intestine is increased, there is more room for nutrients to pass through.

Make a model digestive system
Tell students that the picture of the model is to give them inspiration. They should not just copy it.

Matching the teeth to their function
Point out the example of how to draw the lines to link the picture of the tooth with its name and function.

Modelling teeth
Help students to see the link between the shape of a tool (such as sharp, chisel like or flat) and the shape of teeth (such as incisors or molars).

Taste and colour
Explain that the senses of sight and taste can work together. What something looks like can influence how we taste it and how it is packaged.

Taste survey
Stress that there is no right and wrong in this investigation. Everyone will taste things slightly differently and have different preferences.

Why should we chew our food?

Explain that chewing food has two functions – making food particles smaller and wetter to allow swallowing, and mixing the food with enzymes to start the chemical breakdown of starch to sugars.

Food groups

Point out that the foods that we eat usually contain more than one food group (such as protein and fat in chicken). Foods tend to be richer in one food group than others.

Favourite foods

Point out that sometimes the foods we like to eat are not the healthiest choices. They may have a lot of sugar that makes them taste sweet.

How to design a leaflet

Demonstrate how to fold a piece of A4 paper or card into the various leaflet options. Stress that leaflets give many sections for pictures and text.

Our teeth

Remind students that different teeth have adapted to have different shapes, which carry out different jobs.

Do some drinks damage your teeth?

Explain that pieces of rock are being used because it isn't easy to collect examples of human teeth. The rock is modelling teeth.

Paper plate food chain

Point out that the Sun does not usually have to appear in a food chain. It is added to make the display more visual and to remind people where green plants obtain their energy.

Feeding relationships

Remind students that energy and raw materials are passed along a food chain. The arrows should run from the producer up through the various consumers.

Food webs

Explain that food webs are made by combining different food chains. It is rare that an animal will only eat one type of food source.

Desert food web

Point out the word box. This provides the labels students need to add to the food web.

Make a food web

Encourage students to make up their individual food chains before they start to combine them together into a larger web.

Plants and light

Point out that the labels students need to add to the food web are all included in the word box.

Energy in food chains

Explain that energy is lost along a food chain. Not every bit of energy can be passed along as each animal and plant uses some of the energy up itself. Not all of the eaten food can be digested.

Giraffes and energy

Explain that if a lion only ate one giraffe, then it would be hungry again in days, and would need to eat giraffes throughout its life.

Protecting food webs

Remind students that plants are called producers because they can produce their own food using a process that uses energy from sunlight. Animals are called consumers, as they cannot produce their own food.

How you eat the Sun's energy

Explain that the more stages there are in a food chain, the more energy waste there is before the final consumer is reached.

Protection against predation

Allow students access to the internet and wildlife books and magazines so they can research the methods used to avoid predation.

Adaptations

Point out that adaptations can be physical (e.g. fur colour, teeth or length of legs) and behavioural (e.g. hunting at night, flocking or herding together, hibernation or migration).

4 Electricity

What students will learn

This unit helps students to understand more about electricity and the appliances and devices they use every day. They will learn about the components of electrical circuits and how to identify faults in circuits using batteries. Students will design and use switches, and consider which materials are good conductors and which are poor conductors or insulators. They will also learn about the vital issue of safety and electricity. Students will:

- identify common appliances that run on electricity
- construct a simple series electrical circuit, identifying and naming its basic parts, including batteries, wires, bulbs, switches and buzzers
- identify whether or not a lamp will light in a simple series circuit, based on whether or not the lamp is part of a complete loop with a battery

- recognise that a switch opens and closes a circuit and associate this with whether or not a lamp lights in a simple series circuit
- recognise some common conductors and insulators, and associate metals with being good conductors.

Key words

appliance, battery, bulb, buzzer, circuit, component, conductor, electricity, insulator, switch, wire

Scientific enquiry skills

This unit helps students to develop and practise the following scientific enquiry skills.

Scientific enquiry skill	Page
Ask questions	99, 101, 102, 108, 109
Use equipment	99, 101, 105, 108, 109, 111, 115
Observe	95, 96, 97, 99, 100, 101, 102, 103, 104, 105, 108, 109, 111, 113, 115
Measure	115
Compare	99, 101, 103, 104, 105, 106, 108, 109, 111, 113, 115
Notice patterns	99, 101, 103, 104, 105, 106, 108, 109, 111, 115
Record	95, 96, 97, 98, 99, 100, 101, 104, 105, 106, 108, 109, 110, 111, 115
Carry out tests	96, 97, 99, 100, 101, 105, 108, 109, 111, 115
Group/classify	96, 97, 104, 108, 110, 111
Use secondary sources	102, 106, 113
Communicate findings	100, 101, 108, 110, 111, 113, 115

Ways to help

- Print off large component pictures and their names. Display these in the room.
- Set out a range of components so students can handle them.
- Ask students questions about the appliances and devices they use every day.
- Display large safety posters about mains electricity and cover sockets in the room to prevent experimentation.
- Arrange many broken battery circuits to allow students to practise fault finding.

Helping with activities

The following guidance gives you advice on how to help students with each activity.

Batteries
Arrange a display of battery-powered devices in the room.

Mains electricity
Plan a route around the school or home to allow students to see the many devices and appliances powered by mains electricity.

Wires and circuits
Give students a clue about the mixed-up sentences. Remind them that a sentence will start with a word that has a capital/upper-case letter.

Investigating different materials
Explain that very poor conductors of electricity are called insulators.

Modelling circuits
You could ask each student to draw the component they are modelling onto a large piece of paper and fix it on their front. Then ask them to stand in a circuit to make a circuit diagram.

Components
Remind students that the word 'component' means an object that is part of something else.

Electric music
Explain that a switch is a way of breaking and then making a complete circuit safely.

Make a game
Point out that the 'hand steady' game depends on any touching between the hoop and the folded wire track making a complete circuit.

Open and close switches
Allow students to test their predictions by building and testing the circuits.

Circuits
Advise students to follow a circuit drawing or diagram with their finger to help them detect any gaps. If a circuit has no gaps but is not working, then they should then test each component.

Exploring circuits
Encourage students to look back at their Student Book if they need support in identifying the parts of the circuits.

Drawing circuits
Remind students to include all the listed components in their circuit and check that there are no gaps in their drawing.

Designing circuits

Allow students to move from circuit to circuit to predict if they will work and then test them.

Designing more circuits

Have a pre-made example of the switch so students can pass it round to help them.

Why are insulators important?

Plan a route around the school so that students can re-visit the appliances they found earlier. This time, concentrate on the role of insulators.

Which material is the best for a screwdriver handle?

Explain that the best material for an electrician's screwdriver handle will be an insulator. It will also need to be hard and strong.

Electrical safety

Ask students to share their rules with the class. Ask them to point to electrical devices or sockets in the room as they talk about them to put each rule in context.

Danger!

Allow students to move around the room to place their safety symbols. Then ask students which symbols stand out.

5 Sounds

What students will learn

This unit helps students to understand more about sounds, and how they are produced. They will study the link between vibrations and sound, as well as pitch and volume. Students will also investigate the relationship between the volume of a sound and the distance away from the sound source. Students will:

- identify how sounds are made, associating some of them with something vibrating
- recognise that vibrations from sounds travel through a medium to the ear
- find patterns between the pitch of a sound and features of the object that produced it
- find patterns between the volume of a sound and the strength of the vibrations that produced it
- recognise that sounds get quieter as the distance from the sound source increases.

Key words

decibel, loud, pattern, pitch, quiet, sound, travel, vibrate, volume

Scientific enquiry skills

This unit helps students to develop and practise the following scientific enquiry skills.

Scientific enquiry skill	Page
Ask questions	118, 119, 124, 126, 127, 137
Use equipment	118, 119, 120, 124, 125, 126, 127, 128, 130, 133, 134, 135, 137
Observe	116, 117, 118, 119, 120, 121, 122, 123, 124, 125, 126, 127, 128, 130, 131, 137
Measure	118, 124, 125, 126, 134, 135, 137
Compare	118, 119, 120, 121, 122, 123, 124, 125, 126, 127, 128, 129, 130, 131, 132, 135
Notice patterns	118, 119, 121, 122, 123, 124, 125, 126, 130, 131, 135
Record	118, 119, 121, 122, 123, 126, 129, 132, 135
Carry out tests	118, 119, 122, 123, 124, 125, 126, 128, 135, 137
Group/classify	121, 123, 124, 126, 132
Use secondary sources	119, 121, 130, 131
Communicate findings	119, 120, 121, 124, 127, 132, 133, 134, 137

Ways to help

- Encourage students to learn the key words by speaking loudly and softly. Ask students to tell you which you are doing.
- Set out a range of musical instruments so students can play them.
- Ask students questions about the sounds they hear every day.
- Allow students to act out sound waves by gently pushing each other in line so the wave passes along to the other side of the room.
- Ask students to sit quietly and tell you which sounds are being produced near to them and which are a long way off.

Helping with activities

The following guidance gives you advice on how to help students with each activity.

Vibrations and sounds
Demonstrate how to make the ruler vibrate so that a sound is produced.

Investigating vibrations
Check that the cling film drum skin is fixed tightly otherwise there will not be clear vibrations to observe.

Compose a tune
Allow students to take their guitars home; possibly after practising the tune they will play.

Display information about sound
Remind students to put the number up the y-axis on their graph and the sound sources along the bottom (x-axis).

Sounds in the home
Ask students to discuss which places they find loud and quiet at home and at school before they make their predictions.

Use your hearing to identify materials
Make sure you have a range of wooden, plastic, rubber and metal objects so the sounds produced are different.

Your string telephone
Have a demonstration string telephone available for students to use as a model to help in designing their own.

How does water change the way we hear sound?
Remind students that it is the vibrations in air that we hear as sounds and changing the volume of the air will change the nature of the sounds.

Does distance make sounds fainter?
Ask students to talk about examples of sounds they have heard close by and a long way away before they predict what will happen and carry out their investigation.

Making sounds appear louder
Show pictures of animals with very large ears and ask students if they think these animals will have good or poor hearing. Elicit that catching more sound waves will enhance hearing.

Protecting your ears
Point out that stopping or reducing sound waves from reaching the inner parts of the ear will lower the volume of any sounds.

Survey of uses of sound insulation
Explain that any barrier – walls, doors, glass windows and even curtains – can act as a sound insulator.

How can we change the pitch of a sound?
Remind students that an object vibrating quickly will produce a higher pitched sound. Ask them to think back to their vibrating ruler investigation.

Oscilloscopes
Explain that waves with more energy will be taller than waves with less energy – just like waves in the sea. Louder sounds have taller waves on the oscilloscope.

We all hear sounds differently
Point out that variations in hearing are perfectly natural – just like differences in hair colour or height.

Super hearing at home
Remind students of the giant ears they made in an earlier lesson. Tell them that the ear cone works on the same principle of capturing more sound waves.

Making music with bottles
Explain that this activity builds on an earlier task with the bottles and this time they are going to demonstrate it to people at home.

Making music with glasses
Allow students to practise gently rubbing their finger around the glass – suggest they moisten their finger first. A regular smooth rate will produce the best sound.

1 Solids, Liquids and Gases

Key words

condensation   temperature

evaporation   water cycle   solid

gas   freezing

liquid   melting

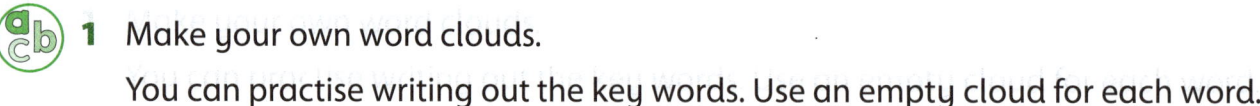 **1** Make your own word clouds.

You can practise writing out the key words. Use an empty cloud for each word.

2 Tick ✓ any words you have used or heard before.

3 Take it in turns with a partner to read out each word.

4 Choose two words. Say a sentence to your partner that uses these words.

Introduction

Examples of solids and liquids

Work with a partner.

1 Look around the room and find as many examples of solids and liquids as you can.

2 Complete the results table.

Name of the object	Is it solid or liquid?

3 What would life be like if everything in the room was made of liquid? Write a short story or poem below.

Are they solids, liquids or gases?

What are solids, liquids and gases like?

1 Complete the table by filling in the gaps.

Property	Solid	Liquid	Gas
Does it have a fixed volume?	Yes		No. It changes to fill the container.
Does it have a fixed shape?		No. It changes to fit the shape of the container.	
How dense is it?	Very dense		
How easy is it to squash?	Hard to squash		Easy to squash
Does it flow?			Yes

2 Write two examples of solids you have used today.

_____   _____

3 Write the names of two important liquids.

_____   _____

Stretch zone

Why are gases easy to squash but solids are hard to squash?

Use diagrams to help you to explain.

Identifying solids, liquids and gases

Look at the list of materials in the table.

1 Is each material a solid, a liquid or a gas?

Colour in the correct box. One has been done for you.

Material	Solid	Liquid	Gas
blood			
carbon dioxide			
copper			
milk			
oxygen			
paper			
petrol			
plastic			
wood			

2 Make up some rules to help you identify which materials are solids.

3 Do the same for liquids and gases, and complete the table below.

Type of material	Rules to help us identify the type of material
solid	
liquid	
gas	

Examples of different states

1 Write the three states of matter.

_____   _____   _____

2 Identify examples of each state.

Fill in the table to record your findings and ideas.

State of matter	Examples I have found	How the particles are arranged

How are the particles arranged?

1 Look at the photographs. Under each photograph, draw how you think the particles are arranged.

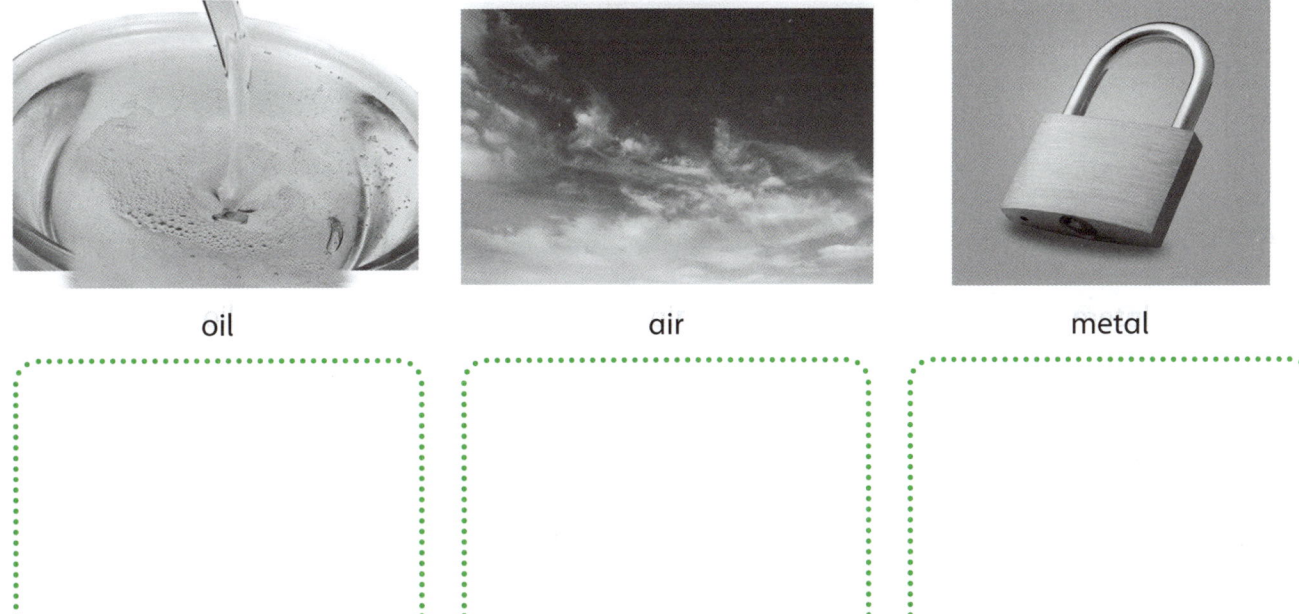

oil   air   metal

2 What are the three states of matter?

_____   _____   _____

3 In which state are the particles closely packed together?

_____

4 In which state are the particles free to move around in all directions?

_____

Liquids

Investigate different shaped containers

 How does the shape of a container affect its volume?

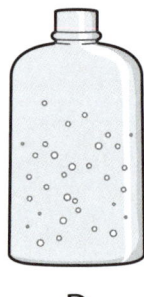

A   B   C   D

1 Predict which container will hold the most water.

I think that container _____ will hold the most water. My reason is:

_____

_____.

2 How can you test your prediction? Answer the questions below to plan your investigation.

What equipment will you need? _____

How will you measure the volume of water in each container? _____

_____

How will you record your results? _____

3 Carry out the investigation. You will test four containers.

What do your results tell you? _____

_____

Was your prediction correct? _____

How can you improve your investigation? _____

_____

How can you get more accurate results? _____

_____

What have you learned about the shape of containers and volume?

_____

_____

Making a lava lamp

You can watch the liquids moving around in this model lava lamp.

If you shine a light behind your lamp, you will get the full effect.

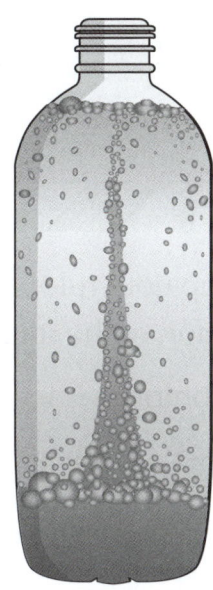

1 Start by adding vegetable oil to the bottle. Stop when it is almost full.

2 Add water to the bottle so it is full.

Observe what happens to the water. Can you explain why this happens?

_____

3 Add a few drops of food colouring to the bottle.

What happens to the food colouring? _____

_____

What happens to the water? _____

_____

4 Break up the antacid tablet so it is in small pieces and slowly add them to the bottle. Observe what happens.

5 Add more antacid tablets to keep your lava lamp moving.

6 The vegetable oil and water are both liquids. Can you explain why the lava lamp works?

Gases

Does air have weight?

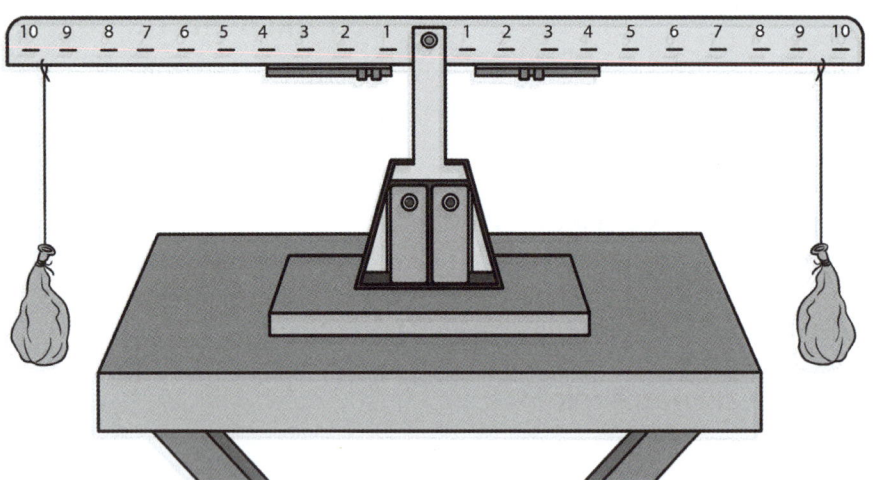

You will need: a ruler, something to balance it on, two balloons, some string.

1 Set up your ruler so that it is balancing on something, as shown in the diagram. Tie a balloon to the ruler at each end.

The balance is level because the two balloons are the same weight.

2 Predict what will happen to the balance if one of the balloons is filled with air.

My prediction is _____

_____.

3 Fill one of the balloons with air and carefully place it back on the balance.

Observe what happens.

4 Was your prediction correct?   **yes**   **no**

 5 Use your understanding of particles to help you explain the results of the experiment.

Adding more particles

1 Place a straw into the open end of the food bag.

2 Close the bag so the straw is held in place and the bag is almost completely closed.

A partner can help to keep the bag sealed around the straw by gently pressing the bag closed.

3 Place the object onto the bag.

Predict what will happen when you blow through the straw into the bag.

I predict _____

_____.

4 Test your prediction by blowing into the bag.

5 What happened? Write a description.

6 Use your understanding of particles to help you explain why this happened.

You will need: drinking straws, a sealable food or freezer bag, a small object such as a book or pencil case.

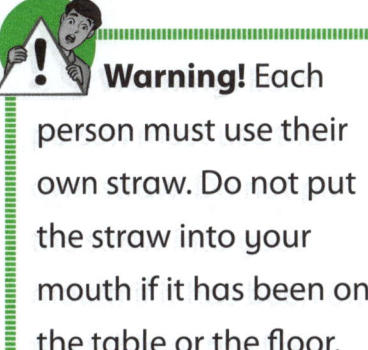

Warning! Each person must use their own straw. Do not put the straw into your mouth if it has been on the table or the floor.

Investigate melting

 This activity supports the investigation on page 25 of your Student Book.

1 Melt some chocolate.

- Place the chocolate in a bowl over some hot water in a pan. Do not heat the bowl of chocolate over a flame or electric cooker.

Warning! Do not touch the hot water or the bowl. Ask an adult to pour the hot water for you. Discuss why this is important.

- As an alternative, you can watch ice cream melting at room temperature.

2 Draw the particles in the chocolate at different stages:

before melting	during melting	after melting

3 Explain how to get solid chocolate or ice cream again.

_____

4 What is this process called? _____

You can use the melted chocolate as a delicious topping for fruit or a cake!

Why salt the paths and roads?

In cold countries the paths and roads can be covered in slippery ice. This is dangerous.

People add salt to the paths and roads before it gets cold because they believe it slows down the forming of the ice.

They also add salt after any ice has formed as they think it will melt the ice.

You are going to test both ideas.

You will need: some ice cubes, salt, bowls or paper plates, two cups, water, a freezer.

1 Collect two cups. Half fill both cups with water.

2 Add a tablespoon of salt to one of the cups.

3 Place both cups in the freezer. Predict which water will freeze first.

4 Observe the cups every ten minutes. Was your prediction correct?

When you are waiting to observe the cups in the freezer you can start the second investigation.

5 Collect two paper plates.

6 Put two ice cubes onto each plate.

7 Sprinkle some salt over the ice cubes on one plate. Predict which of the ice cubes will melt fastest.

8 Observe what happens to the ice cubes. Was your prediction correct?

Now think about the results of both investigations.

9 I am writing to you to explain why spreading salt on paths is a good idea. My reasons and evidence for this are . . .

_____

_____

Heating liquids

Evaporating and boiling

A student has brought home some notes from school. Unfortunately, they have spilled some drink on the page. Some of the words have been washed out.

 Can you fill in the missing words? The words in the box will help you. You can use each word as many times as you need to.

In _____ weather or in a _____ room, water _____ can escape from the surface of water. The water slowly _____ up. The liquid water changes to a _____ called water vapour. This is called _____.

When we heat water, the heat gives the water particles _____. The water _____ move _____ and spread out. When the water is very hot the _____ escapes very _____. You can see _____ forming inside the water. When this happens the water is _____. This very hot water vapour is called _____.

| boiling | bubbles | dries | energy | evaporation | faster | gas | particles |
| quickly | steam | vapour | warm |

Particles and changes of state

Evaporation

Draw a line between each description and the correct word.
One has been done for you.

1 On a warm day particles escape from the surface of water. This is called …	**steam**
2 When water vapour is very hot it is called …	**evaporation**
3 When water is heated bubbles form inside the water. This is called …	**boiling**

States of matter

Complete the diagram.

1 Draw the three arrangements of particles.

2 Write the two changes of state.

3 Write the missing state of matter.

Solid

Gas

Investigating melting

Keep ice cubes cool

This activity supports the investigation on page 29 of your Student Book.

How can we slow down melting?

1 The boxes below have been mixed up. First sort them into the correct order.

2 Then use the boxes to help you plan your ice cube investigation.

Copy the boxes onto paper, leaving room for your answers, and cut the boxes out. Stick them onto another piece of paper in the correct order.

How will I keep my results tidy? Will I use a results table? Will I draw a chart or graph?	**What do I want to find out?** My question is:
What is my prediction? I predict that: My reason is:	**What can I conclude?** Can I see any patterns in my results? Was my prediction correct? How can I make my investigation more accurate?
What will I do? What I am going to measure is: What I am going to do is: To keep safe I will:	**What will I need?** I will need: How will I take measurements? What am I going to change? What am I going to keep the same?

The damaged notebook

This is a page from a student's investigation notebook. They have accidently spilled some liquid onto the page. Can you help by filling in the words that have been washed out?

Use the words in the box below to help you.

We have looked at different examples of _____, liquids and gases. When we _____ a solid it changes into a _____. This is a change of _____. Heating the solid gives the particles more _____. They start to move more quickly.

We also heated liquids. These change into _____. When water changes to a gas in warm weather it is called _____. The gas is called water vapour. If we heat water until it is very hot, _____ is made. This change of state is called _____.

boiling   energy   evaporation   gases   heat   liquid   solids   state   steam

Melting and freezing

Melting and freezing at home

 Are there any examples of freezing, melting, boiling and condensation around you?

1 Carry out a survey to find out.

2 Record some examples in the table.

Warning! Do not go near any boiling materials. Discuss why this is important.

Change of state	Some examples I have seen	A drawing of one example
evaporation		
condensation		
melting		
freezing		

Ice displays

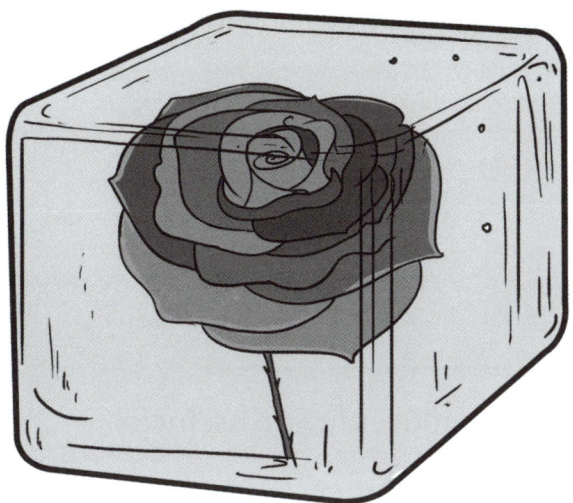 

1 Make a list of small objects that could be frozen into ice blocks.

For example, you could use bottle tops, small toys, flowers, leaves, beads or pebbles.

2 Collect your objects and decide on the three you want for your ice display.

3 Place the objects into empty yoghurt cartons and fill the cartons with water.

4 Leave your cartons in a freezer overnight.

5 Collect your cartons and empty the ice blocks out of them.

Can you see your objects?

Arrange the ice blocks into a display.

 **Stretch zone**

Try to get the objects back out of the ice by:

a chipping the ice away carefully – this is like removing a fossil from rocks

b adding the ice blocks to warm water.

Problems with steam

We have used steam to power vehicles and industry for many hundreds of years.

Write some examples of steam being used.

（blank box）

Coal is a fossil fuel. When it burns it gives off a lot of heat. This makes it very useful for making steam. Coal also produces air pollution when it burns.

An agenda is a list of topics that are going to be discussed in a meeting.

1 Look at the agenda for a meeting.

2 Choose a chairperson. This person will lead the meeting and make sure all the topics on the agenda are discussed.

3 Each person chooses one of the agenda topics.

4 Research your topic. You will be the expert on this topic in the meeting.

5 Hold the meeting and discuss each topic.

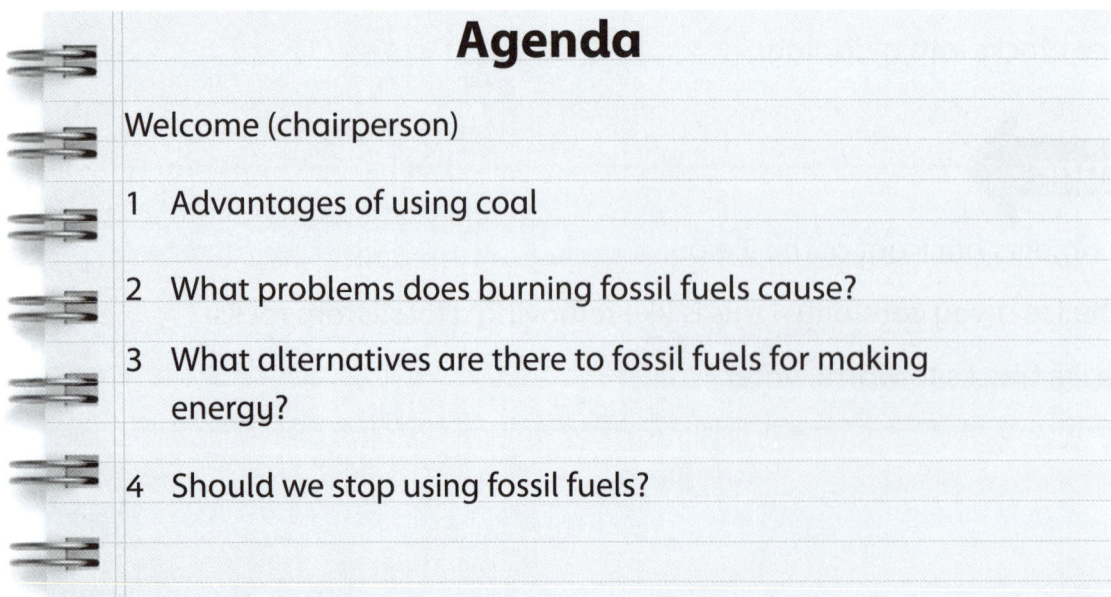

Agenda

Welcome (chairperson)

1 Advantages of using coal

2 What problems does burning fossil fuels cause?

3 What alternatives are there to fossil fuels for making energy?

4 Should we stop using fossil fuels?

Using evaporation and condensation

What happens if someone is stranded in a hot area with only dirty or salty water? It is possible to use changes of state to get drinking water.

When it is hot, water vapour will evaporate from the dirty water. No dirt or germs will travel with the water vapour. If the vapour can be cooled and collected, it will be clean enough to drink. This is what a solar still does.

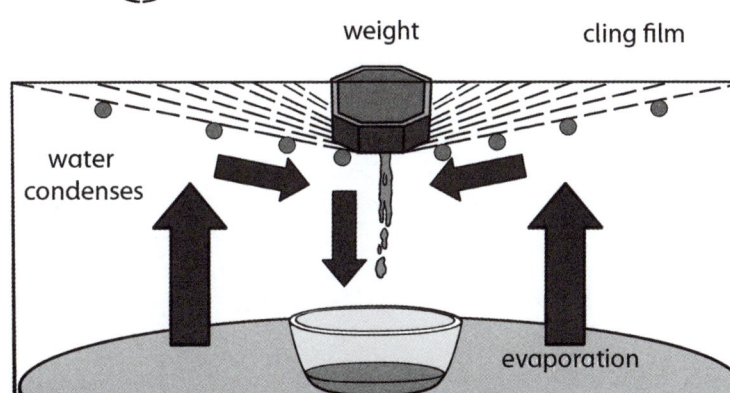

Sun heats water in bowl

weight   cling film

water condenses

evaporation

small bowl

A solar still

1   Set up your solar still. Any high-sided bowl will work well.

2   Add your salty water to the larger bowl.

3   Carefully place a collecting glass into the middle of the salty water.

4   Do not let any salty water spill into the collecting glass.

5   Cover the bowl with a thin plastic sheet or cling film.

6   Place a stone or weight into the middle of the cover – directly above the collecting glass.

7   Leave your solar still in the Sun and observe it every 20 minutes.

8   Did you collect any water in the collecting glass?

9   Explain how evaporation and condensation help the solar still to work.

Warning! Never drink water made from this device unless an adult says it is safe. Use clean water that has had salt added. Never use dirty water for this experiment. What could happen if you did use dirty water?

The water cycle

Changes of state and the weather

The Earth has a limited amount of water. The water changes state as it goes around the water cycle.

The water cycle

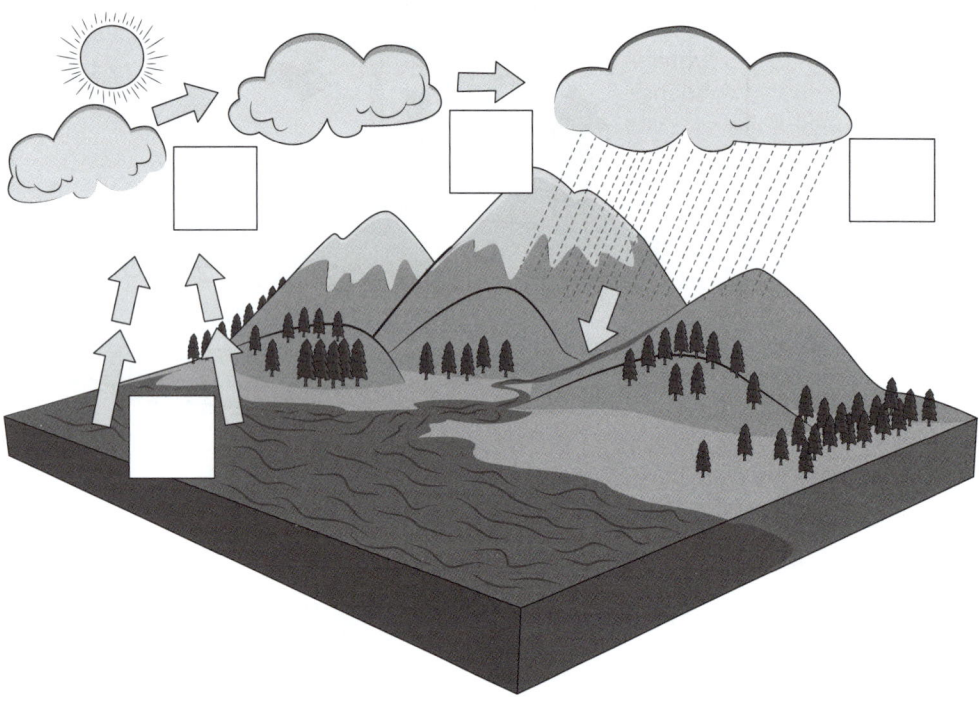

1 Write the letter for each label in the correct box on the diagram.

> **A**   Clouds rise and cool near mountains.

> **B**   As clouds cool the water drops as rain.

> **C**   Water evaporates from the ocean and lakes.

> **D**   Water vapour in the air cools and condenses to make clouds.

 2 What is the difference between pure water and sea water?

Summary of changes of state

1 Complete the diagram showing changes of state. Draw the arrangements of particles in the big boxes. Write the labels in the smaller boxes.

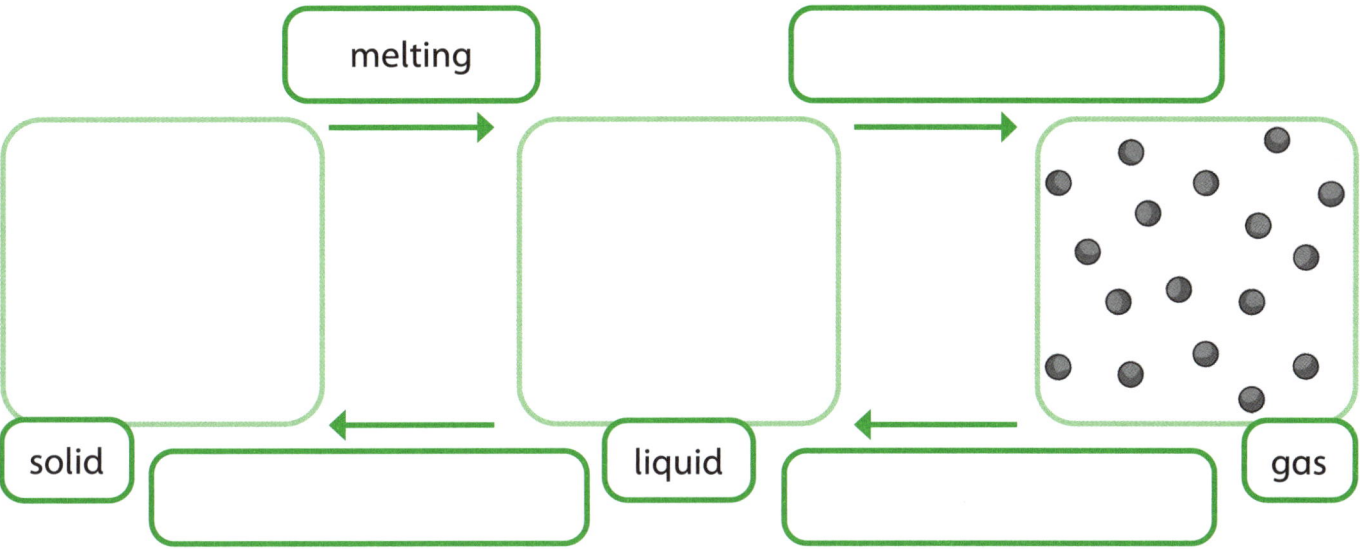

2 Look at these words.

> | liquid | solid | 100°C |
> |---|---|---|
> | 0°C | condensation | evaporation |
> | gas | melting | freezing |

a Draw a circle around the changes of states.

b Tick the melting point of water.

c Draw a star next to the boiling point of water.

d Draw a box around the states of matter.

What I have learned about solids, liquids and gases

 What went well

1 Think about what you have learned.

2 Talk to a friend about something that went well in this unit.

3 Tick ✓ the boxes to rate yourself.

I know that matter can be a solid, liquid or gas.	That's easy. ☐ That's challenging. ☐	Pages 16–23
I know that some materials change state when they are heated and cooled.	That's easy. ☐ That's challenging. ☐	Pages 24–27
I know that melting is when a solid turns into a liquid and is the reverse of freezing.	That's easy. ☐ That's challenging. ☐	Pages 28–33
I know that air contains water vapour and when this meets a cold surface it may condense.	That's easy. ☐ That's challenging. ☐	Pages 34–35

 If you want to know more or need to check, go back to the pages in your Student Book.

Investigate like a scientist

Using evaporation to help make crystals

1 Add hot tap water to the beaker until it is half full.

2 Stir Epsom salts into the hot water. Keep stirring as you do this.

3 Stop adding the Epsom salts when no more will dissolve. You will see crystals settling at the bottom.

4 If you want coloured crystals, then add a few drops of food colouring.

5 Place your beaker in a warm sunny place.

6 Observe the beaker every hour but leave it overnight.

7 Take a photograph or draw any crystals that are made.

Crystals appear as the water is being lost through evaporation. As this happens slowly, the crystals can grow to be big.

You will need: a beaker or shallow bowl, food colouring, Epsom salts, hot tap water.

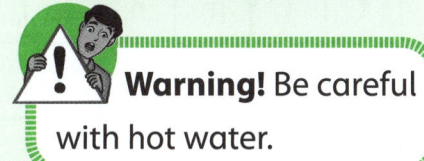

Warning! Be careful with hot water.

Stretch zone

Investigate to see if salt or sugar can be used to grow crystals.

2 Habitats

Key words

 Find the following words in the wordsearch.

> earthquake environment habitat key
> pollution tsunami volcano

Circle each word below when you find it.

m	i	t	u	v	o	l	c	a	n	o	l	e	a
a	r	h	r	c	e	a	p	m	i	a	n	i	t
n	y	i	t	r	e	o	l	n	i	v	y	e	k
o	t	l	m	n	y	h	u	a	i	i	p	t	t
i	a	n	i	m	a	l	t	r	c	p	l	o	o
t	u	k	t	h	o	t	o	u	o	n	a	u	n
u	n	p	a	n	n	n	h	a	r	n	n	p	n
l	l	a	a	a	m	n	t	a	n	a	t	k	v
l	t	m	e	e	n	o	o	t	b	a	i	o	m
o	m	e	n	e	q	n	a	a	n	i	a	o	t
p	l	t	c	s	r	k	r	a	i	a	t	l	p
e	a	r	t	h	q	u	a	k	e	p	a	a	r
l	o	a	p	i	l	o	t	t	e	r	e	i	t
i	m	a	n	u	s	t	i	q	i	k	p	o	o

Introduction

Recording different habitats

Look closely at the map of the world and the photographs. These show different animals living in different habitats.

 1 Which habitats can you see in the photographs? Write the name of the correct habitat in each box. Use the words in the box below.

> desert   grassland   ocean   polar region   tropical forest

 2 What do you think the word 'habitat' means?

_____

_____

1 [ ]

2 [ ]

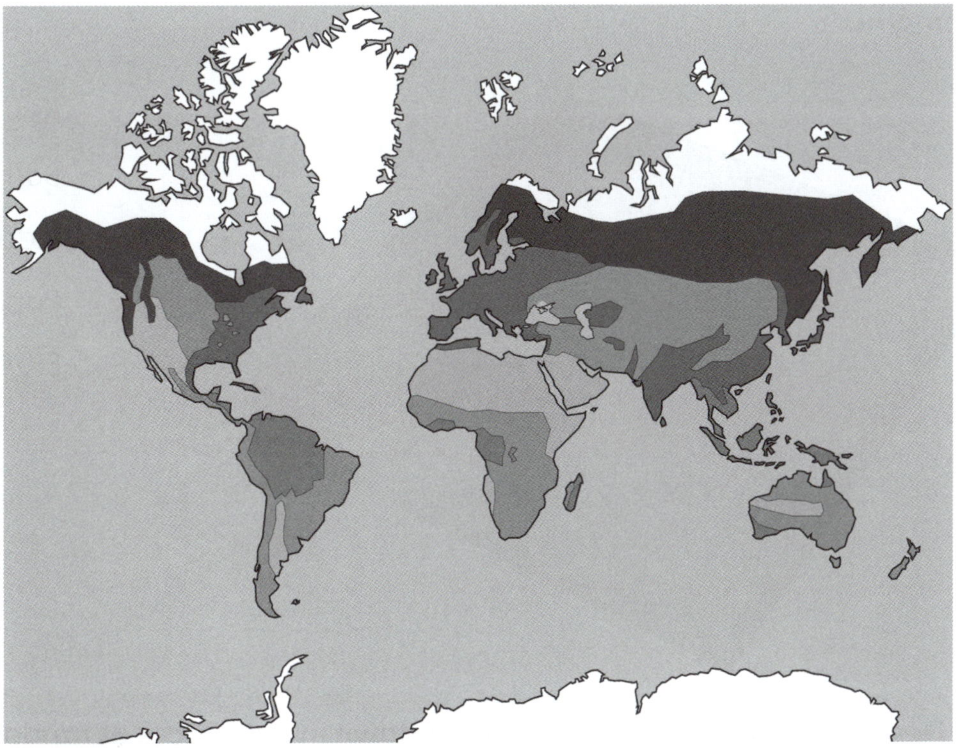

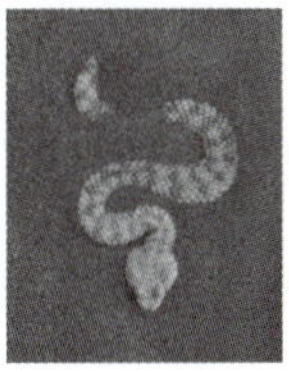

3  [ ]   **4**  [ ]   **5** [ ]

Equipment for investigating habitats

Mini-quadrats

A quadrat is a square that helps us to count animals and plants in surveys.

We place the quadrat on the ground and count the living things inside it.

A quadrat is very useful for counting living things that do not move quickly.

Why is it not so useful for counting living things that do move quickly?

Make your own mini-quadrat using small sticks, such as ice-lolly sticks.

Or cut a quadrat out of cardboard.

Use your mini-quadrat to investigate a sand tray.

Your teacher has placed some objects in a sand tray. The key shows what the objects represent.

Key:

Ball bearings are woodlice.

Pieces of string are worms.

Paperclips are snails.

Erasers are mushrooms.

1 Design a way to place your quadrat down in five places at random.

2 In each place, search for the objects inside the quadrat.

Remember that the objects represent living things, so you must be gentle.

Look at the key to find out which living thing each object represents.

3 Count the number of each type of living thing you find in each quadrat.

4 Record your results. Decide the best way to present your results.

Investigate a habitat in the local environment

 What creatures live near your home?

Ask an adult to help you.

1 Use a mini-quadrat to find out what creatures live near your home (your local environment).

2 Plan your investigation.

- Try to find three different locations.
- How many times will you place the quadrat on the ground and count the living things?
- How will you do this randomly?

3 Carry out your investigation. If you have a hand lens, use it to see small creatures.

Warning! Check with your adult helper that the area you are studying is safe. Do not go near animals that might bite or sting. Some plants can also be harmful.

Use the mini-quadrat that you made at school or make another mini-quadrat using sticks or cardboard.

4 Record your results in the table below.

Location	Equipment used	Living things found	Number of each living thing

5 Take your results into class and compare with your classmates' results.

Investigating a local habitat

Making sense of data

Some students have carried out a survey of living things in a local park. Look at their table of results.

Location	Living things	Number found
Local park	beetles	10
	ants	20
	caterpillars	5
	small flowers	15
	birds	8

1 Show the results as a bar chart.

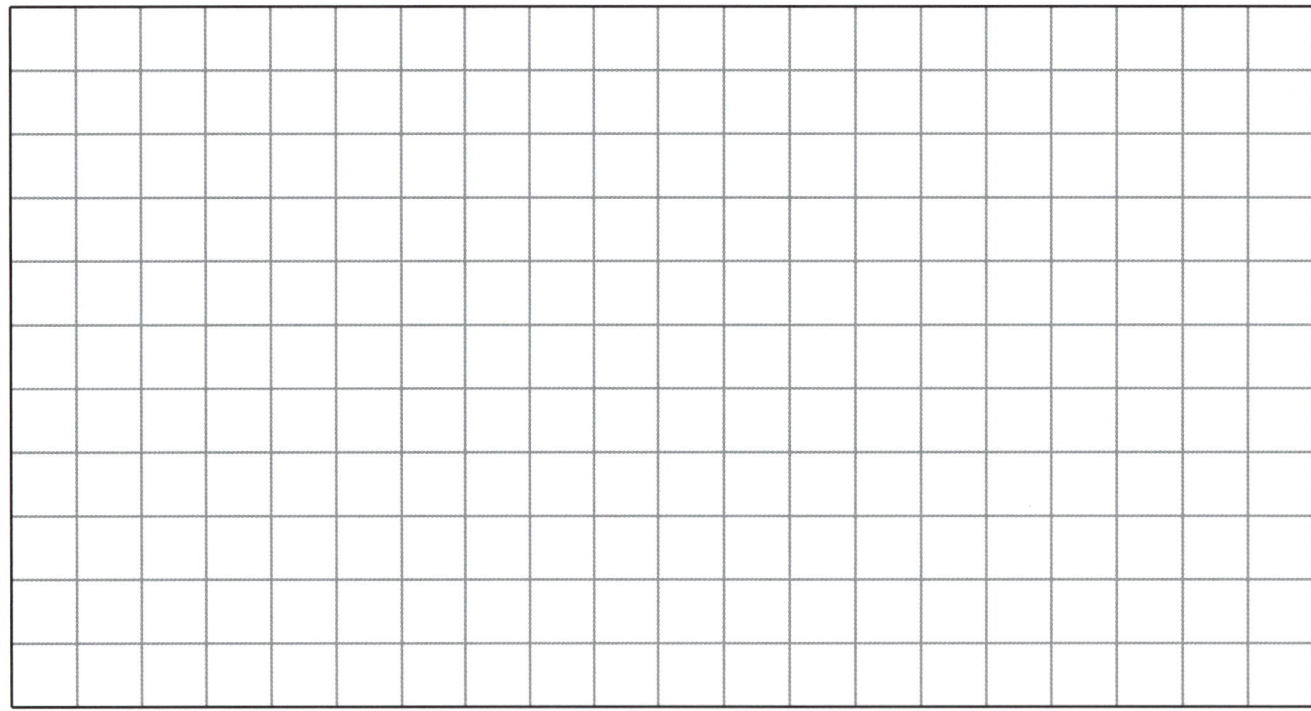

2 Describe two different methods that the students could use to find and count the animals and plants.

1 _____

2 _____

3 Which was the most common animal found in the location?

_____

Design your own animal

1 Invent a new animal. Design your animal so it is adapted to survive in very cold environments and to catch and eat fast-moving prey.

2 Draw your animal.

3 Label the important features the animal has that help it to survive and catch its prey.

4 Where in the world could your animal live? _____

_____

Keeping cool

Animals can become too hot. They need to find cool places to shelter from heat. If an animal stays in the heat, it will lose too much water. It may not be able to get rid of the heat and could die.

 Where can animals keep cool?

Investigate areas around the school to find the coolest places (environments) where animals could survive.

1 Predict the three places where you think the temperature will be the lowest.

These must be natural places and not inside a building or a refrigerator.

- _____
- _____
- _____

2 Use a thermometer to measure the temperature in different places. Try some of the places listed in the box opposite. You can also think of others.

> **beneath soil   in water   on the surface of soil   under stones   under trees**

3 Draw a simple table to record your results.

4 Were any of your predictions correct? _____

5 Which place was the coolest? _____

6 Name one animal that lives in the local area. _____

Adaptations to the environment

1 Choose an animal that lives in your local area. Draw it and write its name. Label any adaptations it has that help it to live in its habitat.

> (empty drawing box)

2 Humans adapt too. Write some examples of how you:

a keep cool in hot weather

_____

_____

b keep warm in colder weather

_____

_____

c keep dry in wet weather

_____

_____

Design a key

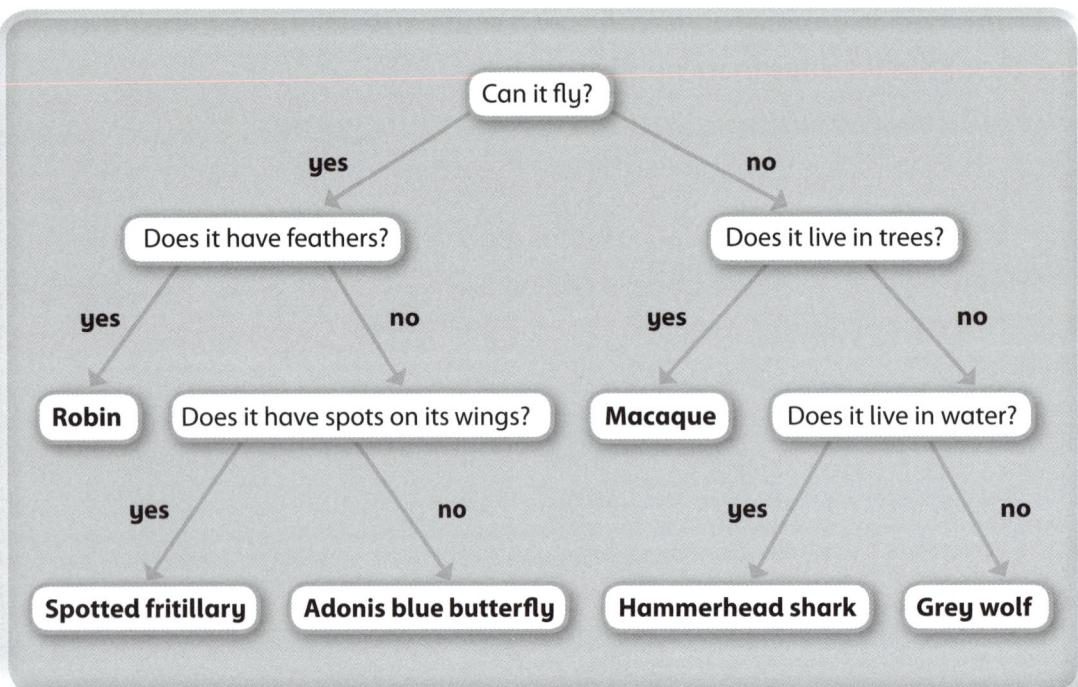

Keys, like this one, can be used to identify different animals and plants.

1 Design a key that will help someone identify whether an animal is a fish, a lion, a lizard or a butterfly.

Remember to ask yes/no questions. For example: Does it have wings? Yes/No

2 Draw your key.

Survey of vertebrates

 This activity supports the investigation on page 47 of your Student Book. You are going to go outside and survey some vertebrates.

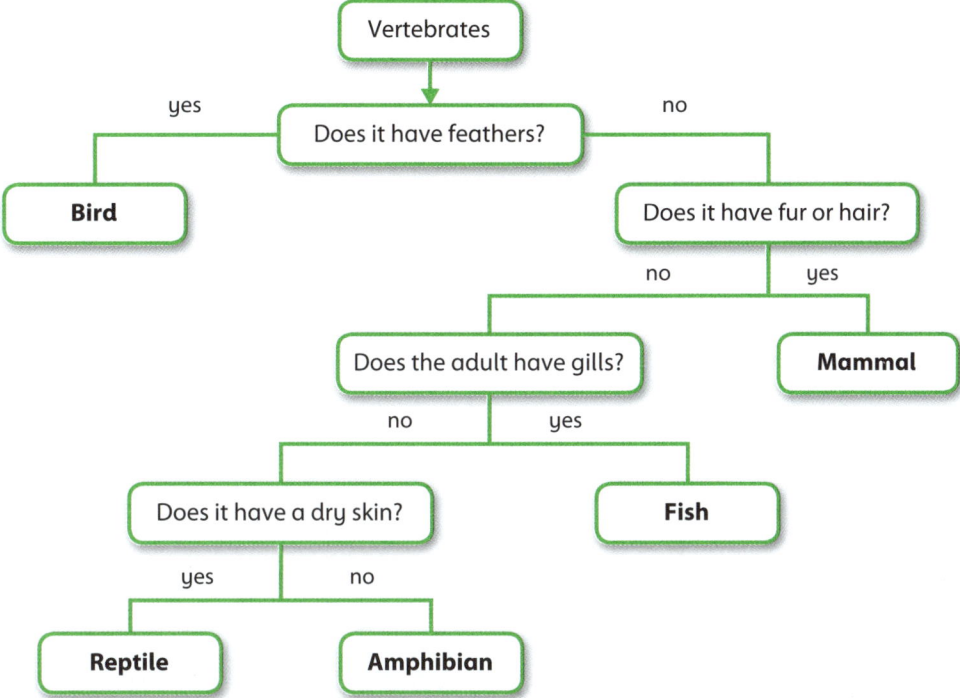

1. Stand quietly. Listen and look for vertebrates. Identify which types of vertebrates you find in your survey. Use the key to help you.

2. Record your observations in the table below.

Class of vertebrates	Numbers seen
fish	
amphibians	
reptiles	
birds	
mammals	

3. Which type of vertebrate was the most common? _____

 **Stretch zone**

Present your findings in a bar chart.

Identification keys for plants

Choosing a cactus for a friend

Imagine that you want to buy two very special cacti for a friend. You know that your friend likes flowering cacti with pink flowers and also round cacti with red spines.

1 Use the identification key below (and the coloured version in your Student Book on page 49) to find the names of the cacti that your friend likes.

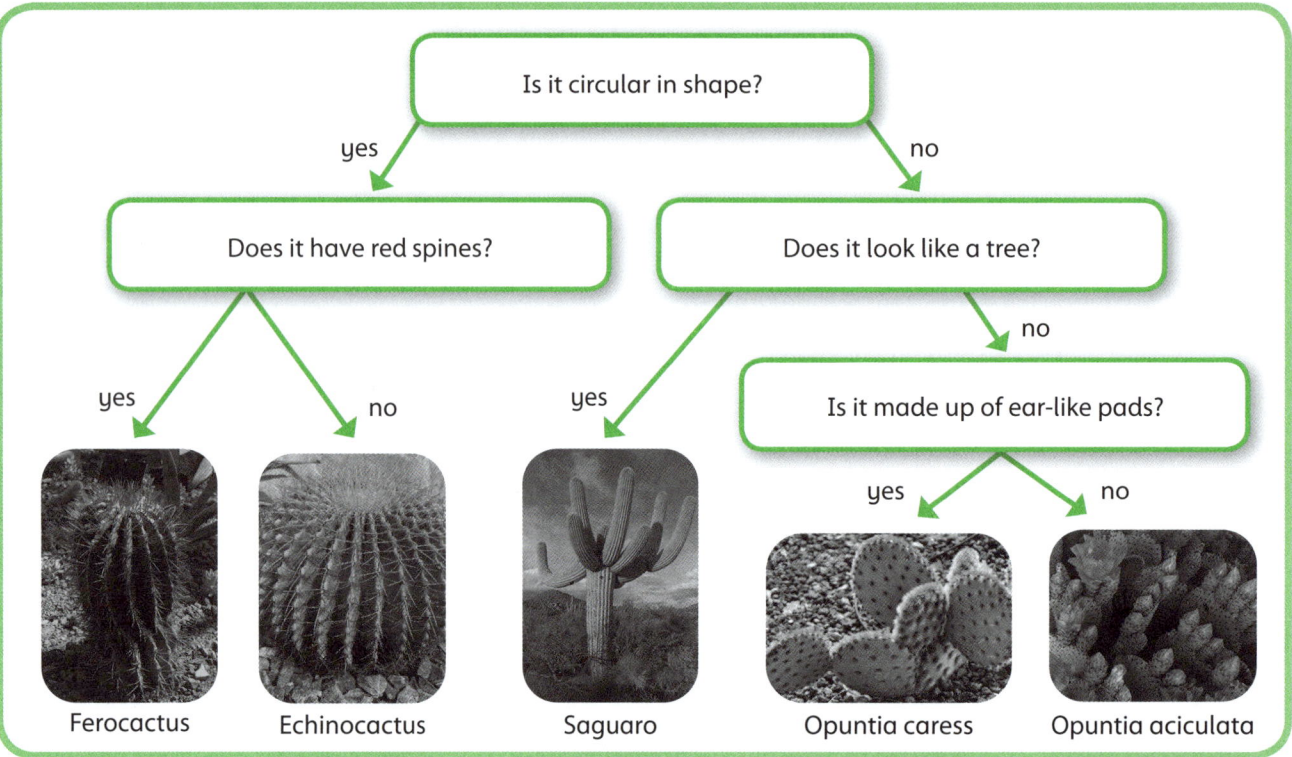

2 The names of the cacti are _____ and _____.

3 Research the cacti and find out:

- the common names for each cactus
- how your friend should look after them.

Florist survey

This activity supports the investigation on page 49 of your Student Book.

Your teacher may invite a florist to talk to your class.

1 Design three questions to find out how the florist learned about plants.

Question 1

Question 2

Question 3

2 How does the florist identify plants? Do they use keys?

3 How many non-flowering plants do they use?

4 How many flowering plants do they use?

5 If you have a visitor, write a thank-you letter to them after their visit.

Include what you have learned about flowers from them.

Fossil fuels

Cleaning up an oil spill

Imagine you work for a group that protects birds.

An oil spill happens when oil leaks from ships or oil rigs into the sea. This makes an oil slick, which can be a big problem for sea birds.

 What problems do you think oil causes for birds?

How can oil spills be cleaned up?

 Investigate different ways of removing oil from water.

You will need: a tray containing water with some cooking oil added, kitchen towels, detergents, sand, more water, spoons, a sieve, some newspaper.

You will work with a model oil spill. You will use cooking oil and a tray of water. Imagine the oil is a large spill of black, sticky oil in the ocean.

1 Plan your investigation. How will you test different ways to remove the oil from the water?

2 Carry out your investigation.

3 What do you conclude from your results?

 **Stretch zone**

Write a short email to the bird-protection group. Recommend the best way to clean up an oil spill.

Researching oil spills

This activity supports the investigation on page 51 of your Student Book.

Make an information sheet about an oil spill you have researched.

Where was the oil spill?

How much oil was spilled?

Describe the impact on living things.

How did people clean up the spill?

Print out a picture of the spill. Stick it below.

Stretch zone

Make a short film or presentation about the spill to encourage people to be more aware of the dangers.

Air pollution

Making an air pollution detector

This activity supports the investigation on page 53 of your Student Book.

You are going to use detectors to investigate air pollution. The plates you make will trap any particles that settle onto them, such as sand, dirt and dust.

1   Take three paper plates. Rub a thin layer of petroleum jelly onto the surface of each plate.

2   Leave two plates in different places outside to test air pollution. Label them A and B.

Warning! Make sure you fix the plates so they do not blow away and protect them so they do not get wet.

3   Leave the third plate indoors where you think there might be some air pollution. Label this C.

4   Check the plates every day for a week. Then complete the table by ticking ✓ the best description.

Plate	Plate is very clean	Plate has some dirt	Plate has a lot of dirt
A			
B			
C			

5   Which plate had the most air pollution? Why is this?

Surface pollution survey

Another way to measure air pollution is to find out how much pollution falls onto surfaces.

In polluted areas a lot of dirt and dust will settle onto surfaces.

In less polluted areas the surfaces will be cleaner.

1   Take a 2-cm strip of sticky tape and place it onto a surface. Make sure the surface hasn't just been cleaned!

2   Peel the tape from the surface. This will lift up and trap any particles of pollution.

3   Stick the tape onto clean white card or paper.

4   Observe the tape with a hand lens. Decide how much pollution was on the surface. Use the key below.

Key:

unpolluted: no dirt is seen on the tape   low pollution: some dirt and dust seen

medium pollution: half of the tape has dirt   high pollution: most of the tape has dirt

5   Use this method to study surfaces in four different areas.

6   Record your results in the table below.

Surface and location	How polluted was the surface?

Warning! Do not work near roads. Do not touch any surfaces without checking they are safe first. Discuss why this is important.

7   Which surface was the most polluted? Why?

River pollution

What impact do activities have on rivers?

1 Write the letter of the correct impact next to the photograph of each activity.

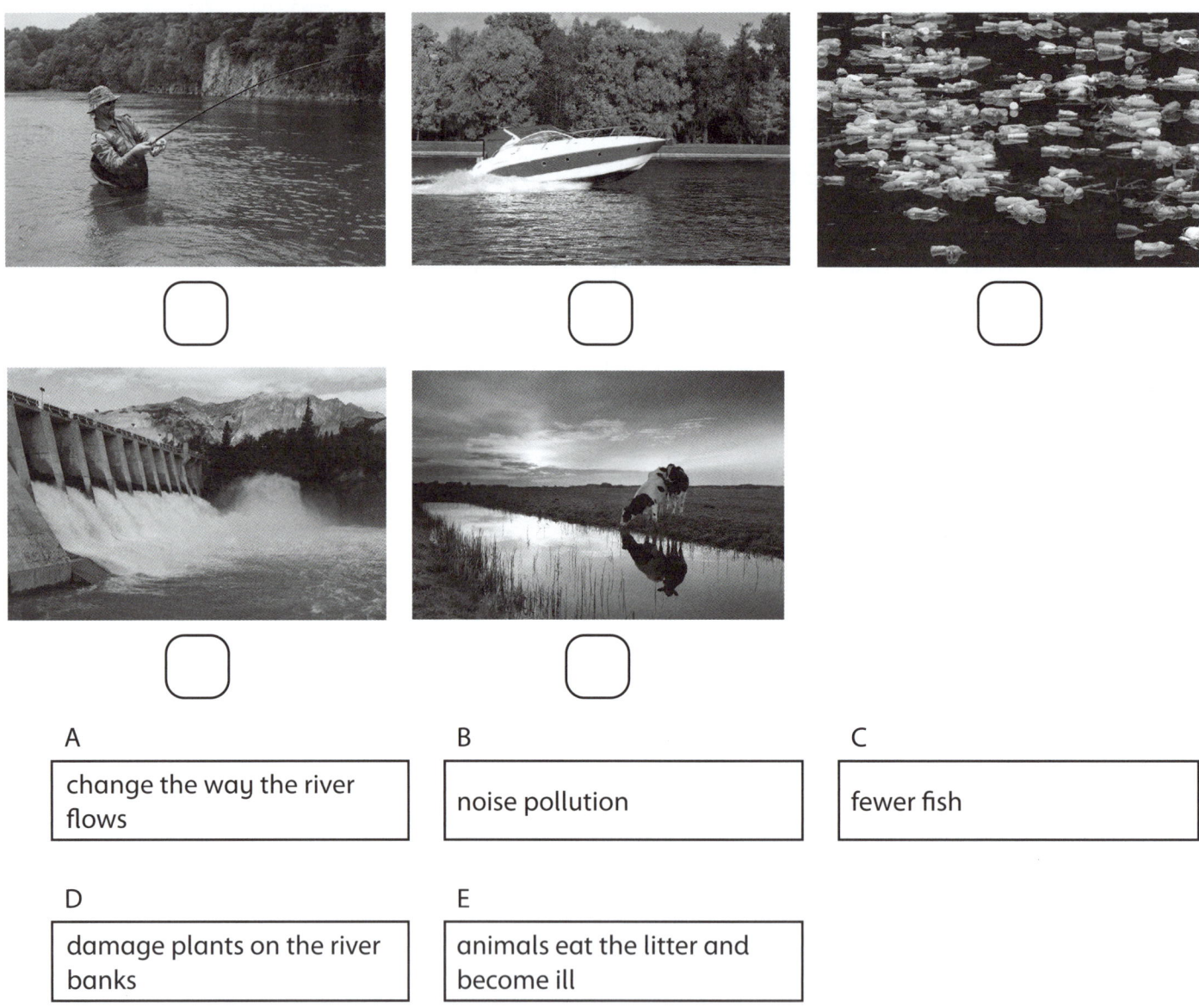

A	B	C
change the way the river flows	noise pollution	fewer fish

D	E	
damage plants on the river banks	animals eat the litter and become ill	

2 Are the following statements true or false? Circle the correct answer.

a Humans use rivers for many different activities. **true false**

b Humans use dams to create energy. **true false**

c Chemicals from factories can harm habitats near rivers. **true false**

d The Amazon is the world's longest river. **true false**

Water survey

How polluted are local waterways?

You will visit a river, stream or pond in your local area.

1 Look for any examples of pollution.

2 Record these in the table below.

Type of waterway	Number of each type of garbage observed				
	plastic	paper	metal	glass	oil

3 Use the following information to help you decide how polluted the waterways are.

Score:

1 = very clean water, fish healthy, no garbage or smells

2 = water clean, some fish, some garbage but no smells

3 = water dirty, no fish seen, some garbage but no smells

4 = water dirty, no fish seen, a lot of garbage and some smells detected

5 = water very dirty, no fish or only dead fish seen, large amounts of garbage and strong and unpleasant smells

Natural disasters — tsunamis

Making waves

 This activity supports the investigation on page 56 of your Student Book.

You will investigate coastlines formed by tsunamis.

Set up your wave machine using a plastic tray.

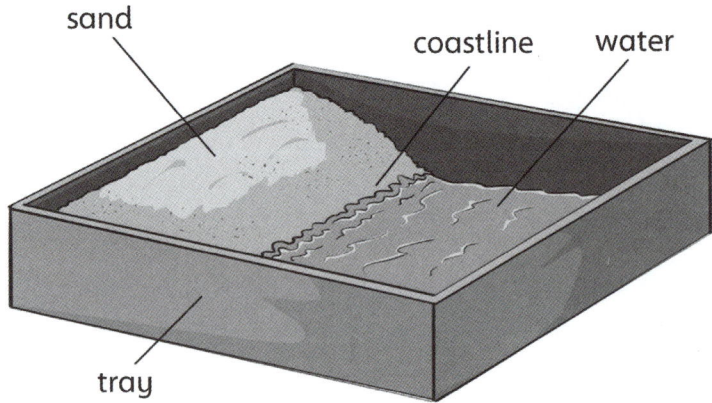

1 Make small houses out of damp sand and stand toy cars near the houses.

   Practise making small waves and large waves.

2 Watch what happens to the sand as the waves hit the coastline and then wash backwards.

3 Make the largest waves you can for one minute.

   Observe what happens to the coastline. What happens to the buildings and cars?

4 Replace any damaged coastline or buildings. Use stones to design a barrier to protect your coastline.

5 Make the largest waves you can for one minute.

   Observe what happens to the coastline now. What happened to the buildings and cars?

Stretch zone

Investigate what happens if the tsunami waves hit the coastline at an angle rather than straight on.

Protecting coastlines from tsunamis

1   Set up your sand tray as you did in the last investigation. Make a small village near to your coastline.

2   Fix a line of twigs and small branches along your coastline. These will represent mangrove trees.

3   Make waves to wash against your coastline. Start with small waves. Then make the biggest waves you can.

4   Describe what happens to your coastline.

5   Did the model mangrove trees help to prevent damage to the coastline?

 6   Think about other ways coastlines can be protected.

Stretch zone

Investigate some of the other ways coastlines can be protected. Present your ideas.

Science fact: Scientists now know that mangrove trees can reduce the power and height of tsunami waves by up to 30%.

Natural disasters – volcanoes

Ash from volcanoes

Use the information in your Student Book to help you answer the following questions. Look at pages 58–59.

1 Label the diagram of the volcano. Draw straight lines from each label to the feature.

ash and gas cloud

crater cone

Earth's crust

lava

magma chamber

vent

2 Describe how a volcano produces lava and ash.

_____

_____

_____

3 What are the problems caused by the ash?

_____

_____

_____

Advantages and disadvantages of volcanoes

1 Study the table below.

Advantages of volcanoes	Disadvantages of volcanoes
Create new areas of land	Health problems, from breathing gases and ash
Make rich, fertile soils for farming	Lava destroys habitats and buildings
Gemstones and metals are found near volcanoes	Explosions can cause loss of life
Attract visitors to help the local economy	Ash and lava can pollute rivers and the oceans
Create black sand beaches	Ash can clog up engines of cars and aircraft

2 Design a presentation about volcanoes. Consider:

- how volcanoes can cause damage
- how volcanoes can also be useful.

Natural disasters — earthquakes

Earthquake-proof buildings

 This activity supports the investigation on page 61 of your Student Book.

You are going to make an earthquake-proof building.

Work with a team to design, make and test an earthquake-proof building.

Your building material will be dry spaghetti or drinking straws.

Building requirements:

The building must be at least 30 centimetres tall. It must hold a 100-gram weight off the ground without collapsing.

1 Discuss possible plans with your team. Decide on the best plan.

2 Construct your building. Fix the building together using glue or very small pieces of sticky tape. You can only use tape to make the joins between straws or spaghetti.

Draw your building.

3 Do you think your building will survive an earthquake?   **yes**   **no**

4 Your teacher will test your building by modelling an earthquake.

The test is to place the 100-gram weight on the building and then shake the table backwards and forwards.

How well did your building survive? _____

5 How can you make your design better? _____

_____

Earthquake safety

What to do DURING an earthquake?

DROP

COVER

HOLD

During earthquakes, drop to the floor, take cover under a desk or table, and hold on to it so that it doesn't move away from you. Wait there until the shaking stops.

1 Look at the safety poster above. Use the information to plan a short play. Your play will show people how to keep safe during an earthquake.

- Decide who will play the different parts.

- Will you have someone explaining what is happening? This is a narrator.

- How will you start your play?

- How will you end your play?

2 Perform your play to show all the ideas.

Think about the advice you have learned.
What are the most important messages to remember?

What I have learned about habitats

What went well

1 Think about what you have learned.

2 Talk to a friend about something that went well in this unit.

3 Tick ✓ the boxes to rate yourself.

I know that living things can be grouped in a variety of ways.	That's easy. ☐ That's challenging. ☐	Pages 40–45
I can use identification keys to group and identify a variety of living things.	That's easy. ☐ That's challenging. ☐	Pages 46–49
I can describe some ways that human impact damages environments.	That's easy. ☐ That's challenging. ☐	Pages 50–55
I know that tsunamis are giant waves that damage coastlines.	That's easy. ☐ That's challenging. ☐	Pages 56–57
I can describe the positive and negative impacts of volcanoes on environments.	That's easy. ☐ That's challenging. ☐	Pages 58–59
I know the dangers of earthquakes.	That's easy. ☐ That's challenging. ☐	Pages 60–61

 If you want to know more or need to check, go back to the pages in your Student Book.

Investigate like a scientist

Making a micro-habitat

You will use a large plastic drinks bottle to make a micro-habitat. This will attract small animals such as snails, beetles and ants.

1 Cut the top of the bottle away to make a larger opening. Place some soil, leaves and stones in your bottle. You could also plant some grass or flower seeds.

2 Lay the bottle on its side in a shady place outside.

> **Warning!** Do not put your hand into the bottle. The cut edges of the bottle may be sharp or there could be stinging or biting animals inside it.

3 Record what you see in the bottle each day for five days. Complete the table below.

Day	Animals found in the micro-habitat
1	
2	
3	
4	
5	

4 After your investigation:

- Carefully tip the soil and plants out of your micro-habitat. This will let the animals find another habitat.

- Reuse or recycle your plastic bottle.

Stretch zone

How would you design and build a habitat to attract larger animals such as reptiles or mammals?

_____

_____

_____

Key words

 Answer the clues to fill in the crossword.

All the answers are key words for this unit. One has been done for you.

Clues:

Down

1 An animal that catches and eats other animals.

2 The animal that is eaten by a predator.

3 These cut, chew and grind up food during eating.

4 This shows what living things eat and what eats them.

Across

5 A plant that makes its own food, helped by energy from the Sun.

6 ~~The system that breaks down food into smaller nutrients.~~

7 The sense that uses sensors in the mouth.

8 An animal that eats parts of other animals.

Introduction

Designed for eating

Study the skulls in the pictures:

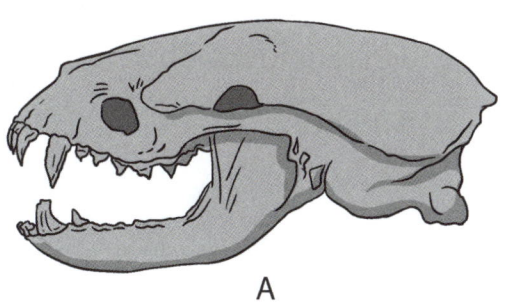

A

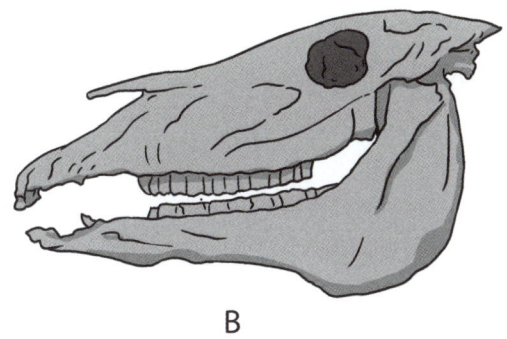

B

C

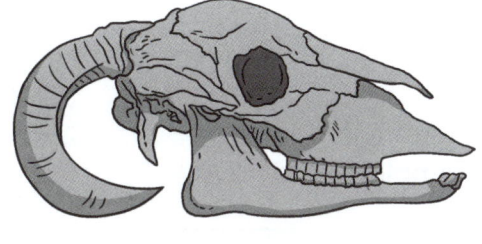

D

1   Which two animals are designed to bite off plants and grind them to make them easy to swallow? _____ and _____

2   What clues did you use?

3   Which two animals are designed to bite into other animals and tear them into smaller pieces to make them easier to eat? _____ and _____

4   What clues did you use?

Breaking down food

Energy in food

You can use the energy in food to heat up water.

The more energy the food has the more the water will heat up.

Two students set up the equipment below. They then tested four different foods. Their results are shown in the table.

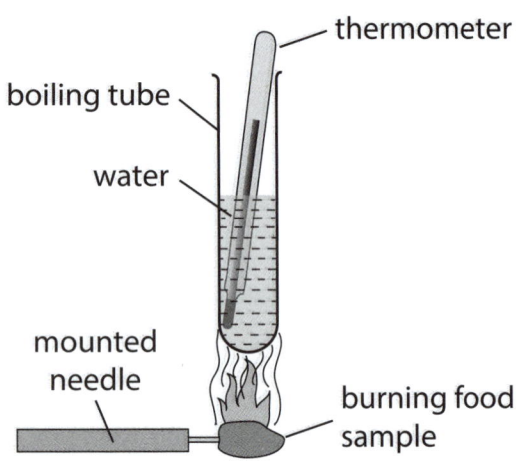

thermometer

boiling tube

water

mounted needle

burning food sample

	Temperature of 20 cm³ of water (°C)		
	At the start	At the end	Temperature change
crisps (2 grams)	25	31	
marshmallows (2 grams)	25	34	
popcorn (2 grams)	25	30	
cheese (2 grams)	25	36	

1 Calculate the increase in temperature for each food. Complete the table.

2 Which food had the most energy? _____

3 Why was it important to use the same amount of food each time?

4 Why was it important to use the same amount of water each time?

Label the digestive system

1 Label the diagram. Use the words in the table.

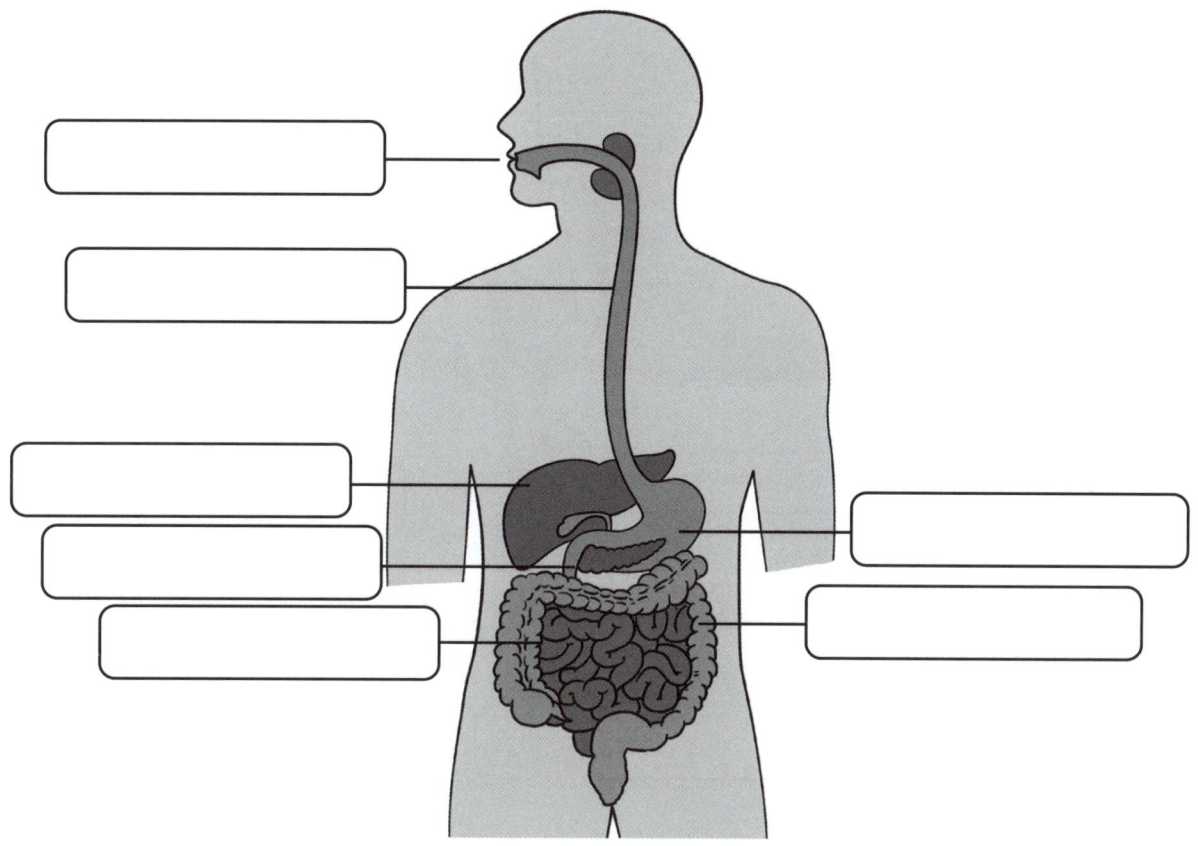

2 Complete the table. Write down the function of each part.

Name	Function
large intestine	
liver	
mouth	
oesophagus	
pancreas	
small intestine	
stomach	

More about absorption

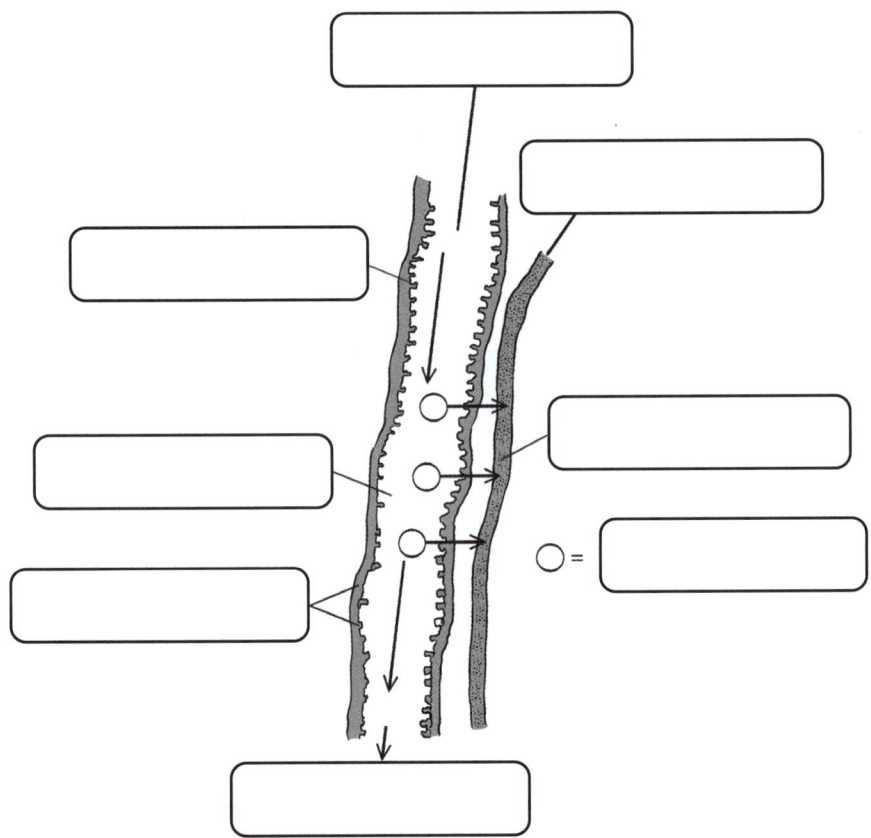

blood   blood vessel   digested food   nutrients   small folds   small intestine
small intestine wall   to the large intestine

1   Complete the diagram by writing the labels. Use the words in the box.

2   Why is it important that the wall of the small intestine has many small folds?

3   Why is it important that the small intestine has a very good blood supply?

Make a model digestive system

 This activity supports the investigation on page 69 of your Student Book.

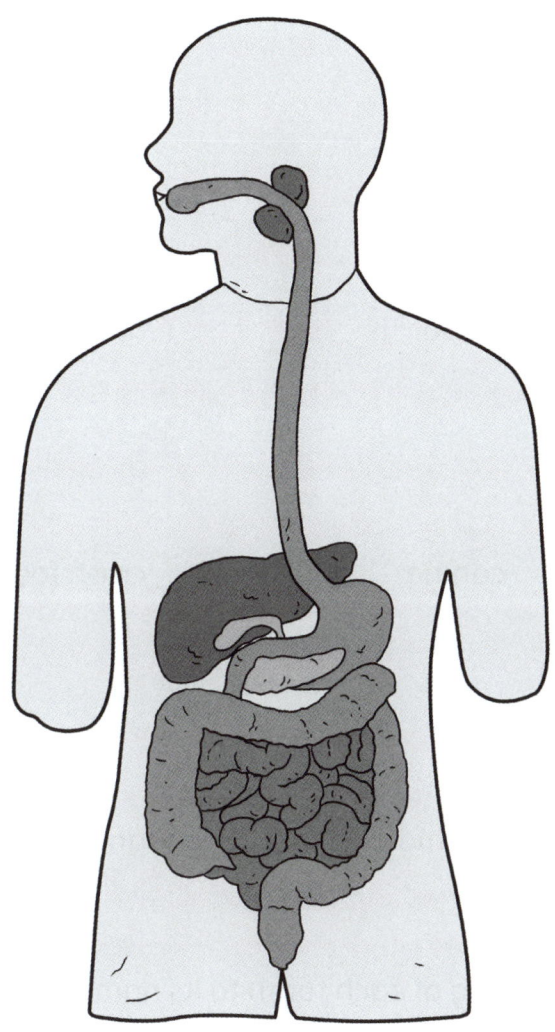

You will use various modelling materials.

1   Plan your model and draw out your ideas. You can use the diagram above to get you started.

2   Make your model. Include all the parts of the digestive system.

3   Make an information label and card for each part of the digestive system.

4   Display your model.

 5   Think about how your model could be improved.

Teeth

Matching the teeth to their function

Tooth	Name	Function
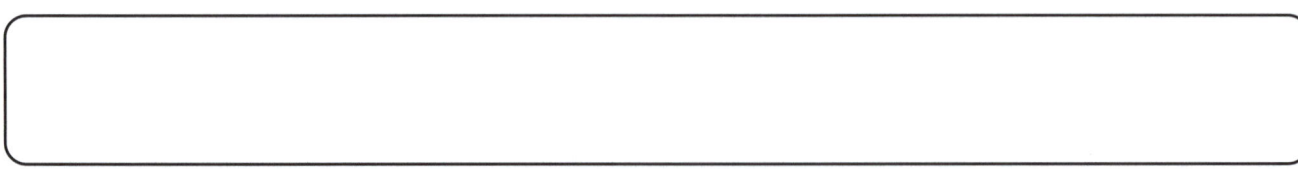	molar	chop and cut food into smaller pieces
	incisor	rip and tear food
	canine	crush food
	pre-molar	grind food

1   Draw a line to link the drawing of each tooth to its name and function. One has been done for you.

2   Explain why lions have large canine teeth.

3   Explain why cows have large molars and pre-molars.

Modelling teeth

This activity supports the investigation on page 71 of your Student Book.

Score:

3 = it easily breaks the food into smaller pieces

2 = it breaks the food into some smaller pieces but it isn't easy

1 = it does not break the food down into smaller pieces

Try to use the different tools to help you break the different foods into small pieces.

The tools represent different types of teeth.

1 Use each tool on each type of food. Give it a score.

2 Record your observations in the table below.

Tools	Foods				
	seeds	bread	soft fruit	celery	nuts
screwdriver					
hammer					
pestle and mortar					
ruler					

3 Which tool represents which type of tooth?

screwdriver = _____   hammer = _____

pestle and mortar = _____   ruler = _____

4 Design a poster display of your findings.

Taste

Taste and colour

 What does it taste like?

Your teacher will give you four cups of juice labelled 1 to 4.

Each drink is a different colour. Can you tell from the colour what the drink will taste like?

1   Look at each drink and think about how it will taste.

Record your predictions in the table.

Drink	Prediction	Taste
1		
2		
3		
4		

2   Use your straw to taste each drink. Only use your own straw.

Record how each drink tasted in the table. Use the words in the box to help you.

> bitter   salty   savoury   sour   sweet

3   How accurate were your predictions? Can you trust your eyes to tell you what things will taste like?

Taste survey

This activity supports the investigation on page 73 of your Student Book.

You are going to carry out a survey of your class. Find out which is the most popular taste.

There are sweet, salty, sour, bitter and savoury foods

1 Predict which foods are most popular in your class.

2 Use the table below to record the results from your survey. You can use tally marks.

Taste	Number of students
bitter	
salty	
savoury	
sour	
sweet	

3 Show the results as a bar chart, using the information you recorded in the table.

4 Which was the most popular flavour in your class?

5 Did your results support your prediction?

Sorting foods into groups

Why should we chew our food?

 Does chewing change the taste of food?

1 Place a small piece of bread on your tongue.

What does it taste like? _____

2 Now chew the piece of bread for two minutes.

What does it taste like now? _____

3 You can swallow the bread or spit it out into a paper towel.

Stretch zone

Bread is a carbohydrate. It contains starch. When you first put the bread in your mouth it tastes different from when you have chewed it. This is because carbohydrates are made of very big units. When you chew the bread it mixes with your saliva. A material in the saliva called amylase breaks the units up. The smaller units are sugar. This is why the bread tastes sweeter after you have chewed it.

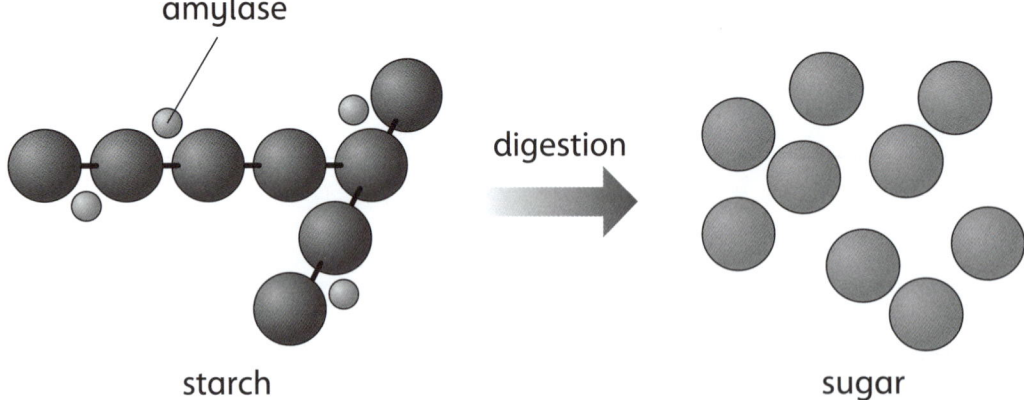

Can you list any other reasons for chewing your food?

_____

_____

Food groups

carbohydrates   fats   proteins   vitamins

1 Copy the different words into each of the boxes above.

2 Draw pictures of examples of each food group in the boxes.

3 Compare your food examples with others. Did anyone use a food example for a different taste group?

Unhealthy foods

Favourite foods

Are people's favourite foods healthy?

1 Choose three people to help you with a survey about favourite foods.

2 Ask each person the three questions and complete the table.

3 Ask yourself the questions as well and write your answers in the table.

1 Name your five favourite foods.

2 How often do you eat sweets, cakes or chocolate in a day?

3 How often do you eat fruits and vegetables in a day?

Person's name	1 Five favourite foods	2 Number of times they eat sweets, cake or chocolate	3 Number of times they eat fruits and vegetables

4 Which favourite foods are the healthiest? _____

_____

5 Who eats the most carbohydrates? _____

6 Who eats the most fruits and vegetables? _____

How to design a leaflet

1 Design a leaflet for a hospital waiting room. Include all the facts you have learned about exercise and healthy eating.

2 Explain why adults should exercise and eat healthily to avoid obesity.

3 Draw pictures to make your leaflet eye-catching.

Different ways to fold a leaflet

Remember:

- look at other leaflets for ideas

- have a clear title

- make the information stand out

- check that the information is correct.

Looking after teeth

Our teeth

We have different types of teeth to help us eat our food.

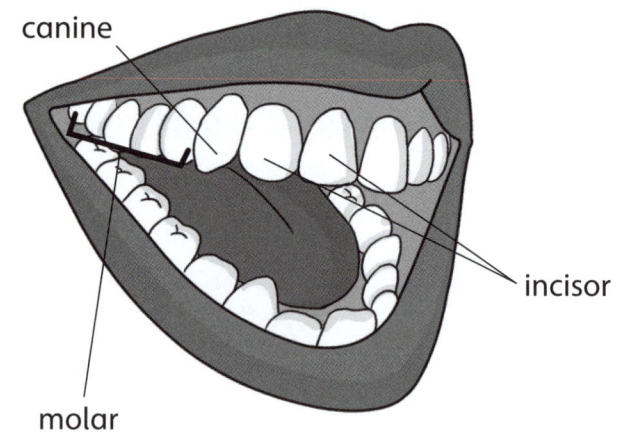

- Incisors are at the front. They have sharp edges like scissors. They help us to bite food into smaller pieces.

- Canines are near the front. They are pointed. They help us to grip and tear our food.

- Molars are at the back. They are flat. They help us to grind and chew our food.

1 Lions have large canine teeth. Why?

_____

2 Cows have large molars. Why?

_____

3 Look at your own teeth. You may still have your milk teeth. These will fall out to be replaced with adult teeth. The adult teeth are not replaced again so you will need to look after them!

Write three ways you can look after your teeth.

1 _____

2 _____

3 _____

4 Name three foods that you would not be able to eat easily if you did not have teeth.

1 _____ **2** _____ **3** _____

Do some drinks damage your teeth?

1   Weigh four pieces of marble or limestone.

2   Record the weight (mass) in the table below.

3   Place the pieces of rock into the following drinks: apple juice, cola, lemonade, water. Leave them for two weeks. The rocks are made of a similar material to your teeth. Predict what you think will happen to them.

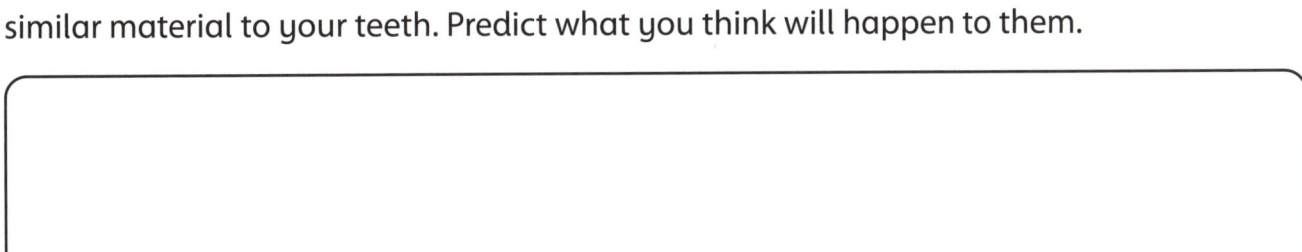

4   After two weeks, take each piece of rock out of the drink. Dry it. Observe each rock piece.

5   Weigh each rock piece. Record the weight (mass) in the table below.

Name of drink	Weight (mass) of rock before leaving it in the drink (grams)	Weight (mass) after leaving it in the drink (grams)
apple juice		
cola		
lemonade		
water		

6   Explain what happened to the pieces of rock.

7   What does your investigation tell you about what some liquids can do to teeth?

Food chains

Paper plate food chain

1 Draw the food chain in the correct order.

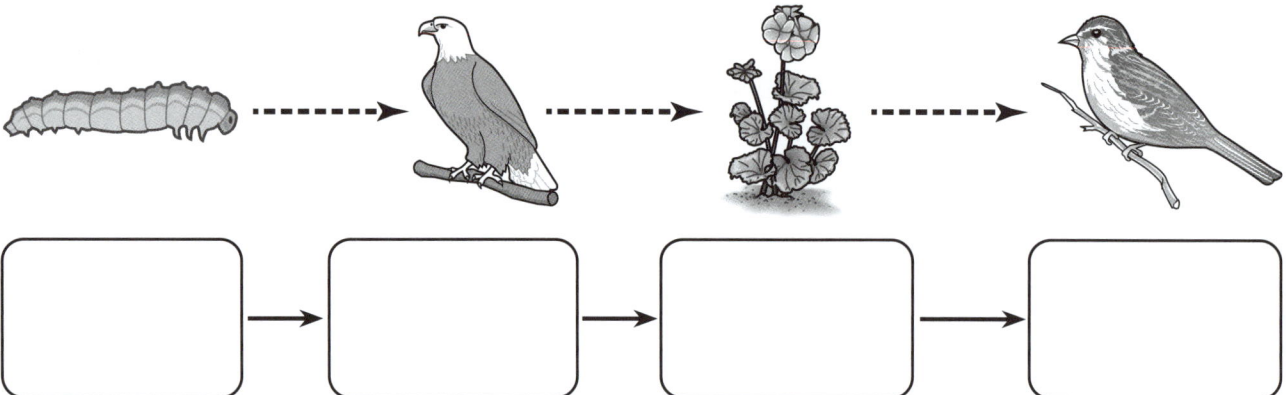

2 Design your own food chain.

3 Use paper plates to make a model of your food chain. Draw the animals and plants on the plates and label them. Place the plates in order. Make cardboard arrows to show the links between the parts of your food chain.

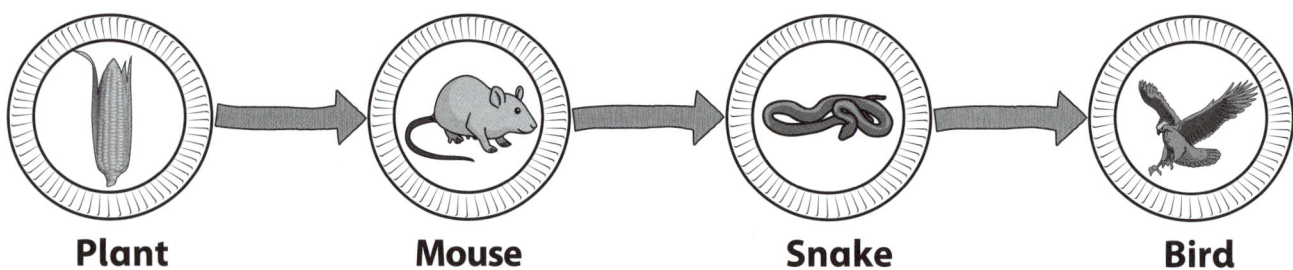

| **Plant** | **Mouse** | **Snake** | **Bird** |

Your teacher will display the food chains next to each other.

4 Compare the food chains.

a What do they have in common?

_____

_____

b How are they different?

_____

_____

Feeding relationships

1 Use the pictures to construct three different food chains. Include one food chain that is under the sea. Write the letters of the pictures in the boxes.

Food chain 1

Food chain 2

Food chain 3

2 Cut out pictures of plants and animals to make your own food chain.

3 Stick the pictures in the box and label them. Draw arrows to show the feeding relationships.

Use some magazines that have pictures of plants and animals, or ask for permission to download pictures from the internet.

Making food webs

Food webs

1 Draw the arrows to show the feeding relationships in this food web. The web should show all the different things that animals eat in their habitat.

Complete the missing labels for some of the animals.

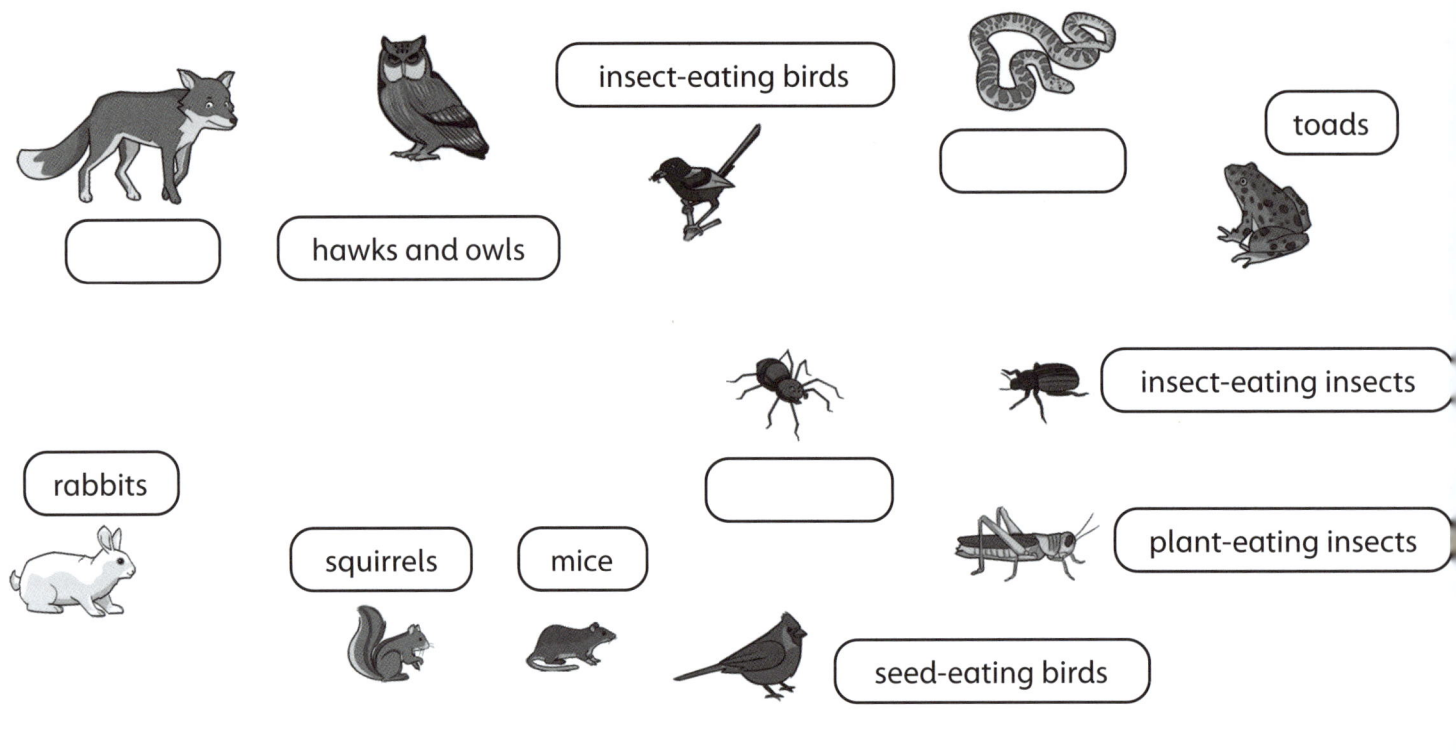

plant leaves, roots, stems, fruits and seeds

2 Predict what will happen to the living things in the food web if the seed-eating birds all die out.

_____

_____

Desert food web

1 Look at this food web.

> **birds of prey   cacti   desert plants
> foxes   insects   lizards   ~~rats~~
> scorpions   snakes**

a Write the names of the plants and animals in this food chain in the boxes. Use the words from the box. One has been done for you. Some words are used more than once.

b Where will you put the arrows? Draw in the arrows to show all the different feeding relationships. One has been done for you.

2 True or false? Circle the correct answer.

a Food webs and food chains give information about feeding relationships.

true   false

b We use arrows to show us what each animal eats.

true   false

c Food webs give more information than food chains.

true   false

rats

Green plants and sunlight

Make a food web

1 Think about a local habitat, for example, a field, a woodland area or a pond.

2 Write three food chains that you might find in this habitat. Use words instead of drawings.

> **Remember:** Include a producer at the beginning of each food chain. Include arrows to show the direction that energy travels along the chain.

Food chain 1 _____

Food chain 2 _____

Food chain 3 _____

3 Join your food chains together to make a single food web. Use words instead of drawings. Include arrows to show the feeding relationships in your food web.

4 Identify one animal that eats the producers from your web.

_____

5 What will happen to the producers if this animal dies out?

_____

Plants and light

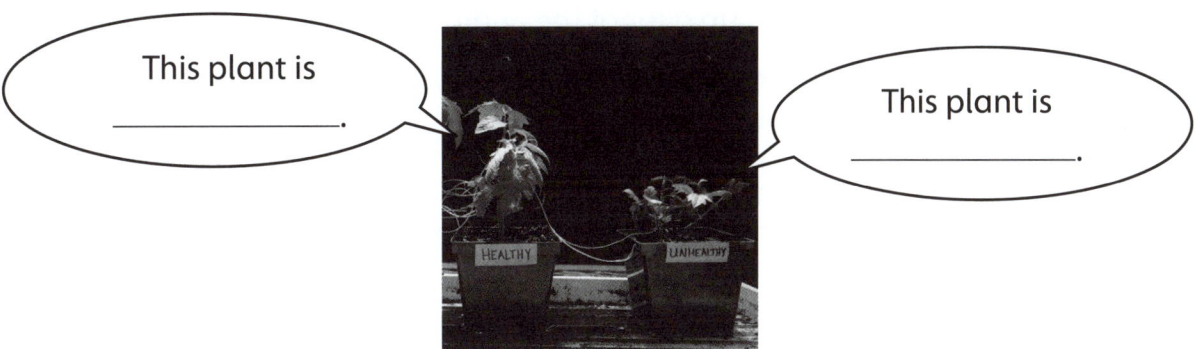

This plant is _____.

This plant is _____.

HEALTHY

UNHEALTHY

1 Look at the photograph of a healthy plant and an unhealthy plant.

   a Write in the speech bubbles which plant is healthy and which plant is unhealthy.

   b What do you notice about the healthy plant? What do you notice about the unhealthy plant?

2 Fill in the gaps in the paragraph below. Use the words in the box.

A healthy plant has _____ but the unhealthy plant has

_____. The healthy plant has _____

but the unhealthy plant has _____. The healthy

plant has _____ but the unhealthy plant has

_____.

> **discoloured green leaves**   **green leaves**   **new leaves growing**
> **no new leaves growing**   **upright leaves**   **wilted leaves**

Passing energy along

Energy in food chains

When an animal eats plants it uses up a lot of the energy. This is because it moves around and produces heat. Anything that eats this animal only gets a small amount of the energy that was in the plants.

Energy is lost at each level in a food chain.

Energy loss in the food chain

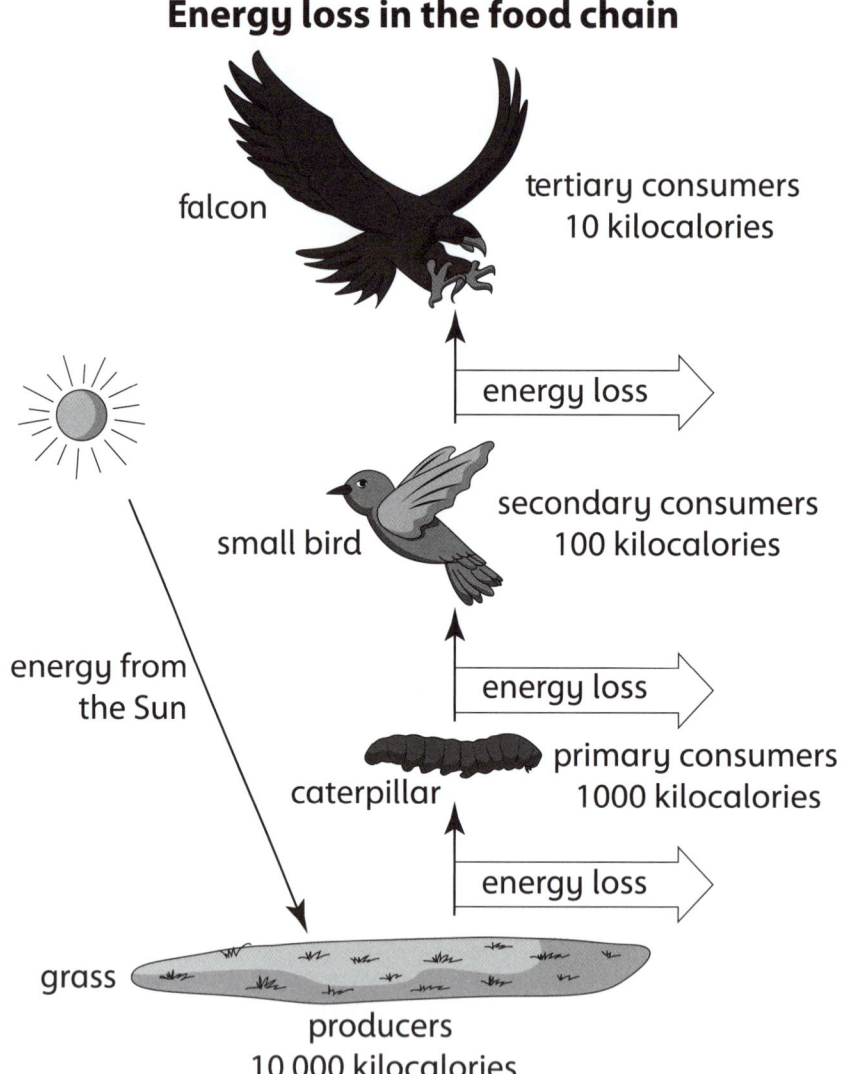

falcon — tertiary consumers 10 kilocalories

energy loss

small bird — secondary consumers 100 kilocalories

energy from the Sun

energy loss

caterpillar — primary consumers 1000 kilocalories

energy loss

grass — producers 10 000 kilocalories

1 What percentage of energy is lost when an animal eats a producer?

2 What percentage of energy is lost when an animal eats a small bird?

Giraffes and energy

1 Look at page 86 in your Student Book. Why does a lion need to eat many giraffes during its life?

_____

2 Write down one reason why giraffes need a lot of energy.

_____

3 Giraffes eat plants. Where do the plants get their energy?

_____

Stretch zone

4 Complete the crossword using the clues below. One has been done for you.

	1									2 s		3	
										u			
							4			n			
										l			
										i			
										g			
										h			
										t			

Clues:

1 Green plants are called this. (9)

2 ~~Plants use this to make their own food. (8)~~

3 The name of the shape showing energy flow. (7)

4 Animals eat food so they can get this. (6)

Protecting food webs

1 Draw a line from each animal to its source of food.

2 What do we call animals that eat only plants? _____

3 How do plants get their food? _____

4 What will happen to the plant-eating animals if all of the plants on Earth die?

_____

5 What will then happen to the carnivores on Earth?

_____

6 Why should we protect the plants that live on Earth?

_____

How you eat the Sun's energy

1 In boxes A and B below, make two food chains with yourself in them. In each food chain:

- decide whether you are a primary consumer, a secondary consumer or a tertiary consumer
- draw arrows to show how the energy from the Sun reaches you
- label the producer and the different types of consumer.

In box **A**, draw a food chain that shows you eating plant materials.

A

In box **B**, draw a food chain that shows you eating meat or fish. If you are vegetarian, include dairy products such as cheese or milk.

B

2 **a** In which food chain did you get the most energy from the Sun? ☐

b Explain why. _____

_____

Protection against predation

Animals and plants have changed in many different ways to try to avoid being eaten.

1 How are these living things protecting themselves from being eaten?

_____

_____

2 Look at the words in the box. They relate to different features or methods that living things use to protect themselves from being eaten (from becoming prey).

> camouflage   flight   jumping   poison   shells   size   sound   speed   spines

Your teacher will ask you to research one of these methods of protection.

Plan and produce a poster to tell people what you have found out.

- Include pictures of some living things that use this method of protection.
- Give some examples of animals that hunt these living things (the predators).
- Explain how the method works as protection.

Adaptations

1 Label the adaptations of the cheetah that help it to hunt prey.

2 Label the adaptations of the gazelle that help it to escape prey.

3 Study the photographs below.

Arctic foxes are predators. They try to catch prey, such as snowshoe hares. In winter, both animals have white coats.

a How else are arctic foxes adapted to be predators?

b How are snowshoe hares adapted to decrease the chance they will become prey?

What I have learned about digestion and food chains

 What went well

1 Think about what you have learned.

2 Talk to a friend about something that went well in this unit.

3 Tick ✓ the boxes to rate yourself.

I know the simple functions and parts of the human digestive system.	That's easy. ☐ That's challenging. ☐	Pages 66–69
I can identify the different types of human teeth and their functions.	That's easy. ☐ That's challenging. ☐	Pages 70–71
I know the human senses and how we use them.	That's easy. ☐ That's challenging. ☐	Pages 72–75
I know that some foods can damage our health.	That's easy. ☐ That's challenging. ☐	Pages 76–79
I know how food chains can be used.	That's easy. ☐ That's challenging. ☐	Pages 80–87
I understand the terms producer, consumer, predator and prey.	That's easy. ☐ That's challenging. ☐	Pages 88–91

 If you want to know more or need to check, go back to the pages in your Student Book.

Investigate like a scientist

Survey of food chains

You are going to carry out a food chain survey.

1 Design your own feeding station to attract small animals and some larger animals. Use the picture to help you.

2 Set up your feeding station. Place it near a flower bed and some trees. Observe it for 30 minutes every day for five days.

3 Record what eats the seeds and plants. Note any animals that eat the smaller animals – such as birds taking caterpillars or beetles. Complete the table.

Day	Animals seen eating plants	Animals seen eating other animals
1		
2		
3		
4		
5		

4 Show one of the feeding relationships you have seen as a food chain.

- Remember to start with a plant. Draw each living thing in the chain.

- Label your food chain to show the producer, the herbivore and a carnivore.

Key words

 Read the words in each of the boxes. Then answer the questions below.

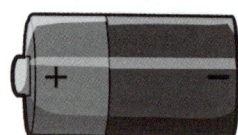

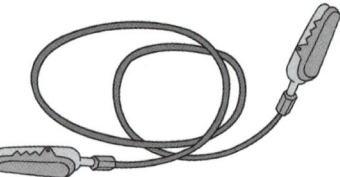

1 Draw a picture of something that uses batteries.

2 Draw a picture of something that uses a wire.

Introduction

Electricity and how we use it

1 **a** Join the dots together to make the word in the speech bubble below.

   b Read aloud the word to your partner.

   c Listen to them read the word out loud.

   d Try to air-write the word.

   e Now write the word on a whiteboard or chalkboard.

   Keep trying until you can remember how to spell the word.

2 What do you know about this word? How do we use electricity in everyday life?

Draw pictures or write words around the speech bubble to record what you know about electricity and how we use it. An example has been done for you.

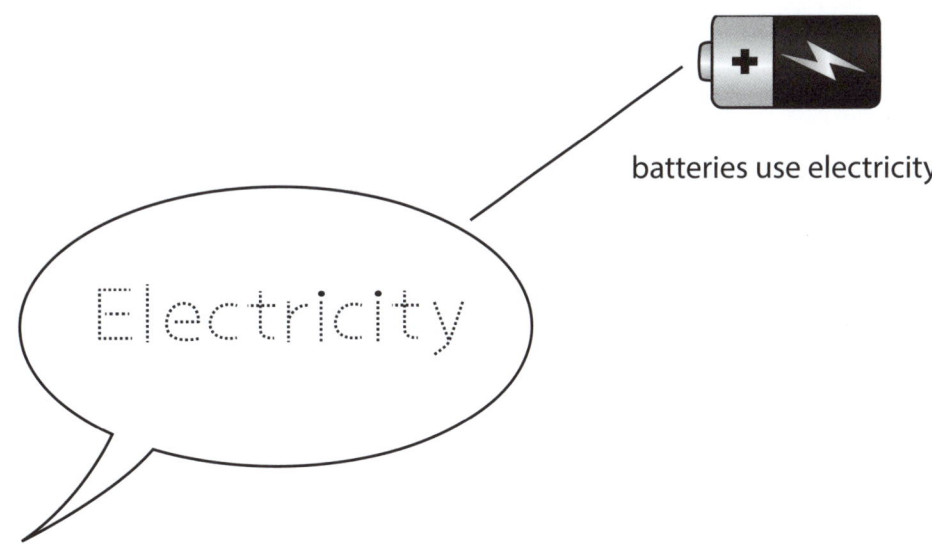

batteries use electricity

Electricity

Electricity supply

Batteries

We use electricity every day. Batteries provide us with electricity.

1 How many things can you find that use batteries?

Record in the table what you find. Take photographs, draw pictures or write the words. An example has been done for you.

2 Complete the sentence by writing the number of things you found.

I found _____ things that use batteries.

Mains electricity

1 How many things can you find that use mains electricity?

The picture on the right gives you a clue.

Record in the table what you find. Take photographs, draw pictures or write the words. An example has been done for you.

2 Complete the sentence by writing the number of things you found.

I found _____ things that use mains electricity.

Wires and circuits

This student is confused about why we need wires.

She has mixed up the words in the sentences.

 Can you help her to understand? Rearrange the words and write two sentences.

| carry | Wires | a |

| from | electricity | battery |

a _____

| electricity | the | carry |

| from | mains | Wires |

b _____

Investigating different materials

This activity supports the investigation on page 99 of your Student Book.

Some materials help the electricity to flow through them easily. Others don't.

You are going to investigate different materials using a simple circuit like the one in the diagram.

1 Set up a circuit like the one opposite. Leave two connectors free so that you can connect different materials to the circuit.

If the bulb lights, the material you connect to the connectors is letting the flow of electricity through.

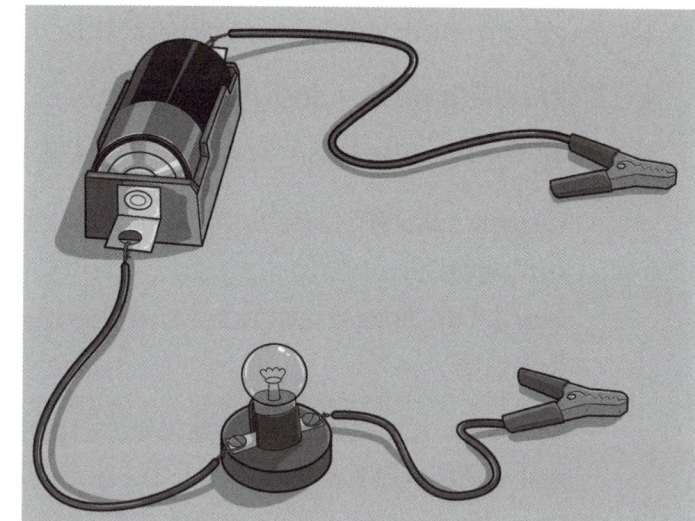

2 Use the table to help you record your predictions and results.

Write the name of the material in the first column.

3 Draw a tick ✓ in the prediction column if you think it will light the bulb.
Draw a cross ✗ if you think the bulb will not light.

4 Carry out your tests and use ticks and crosses in the results column. You could use more ticks if the bulb is brighter.

An example has been done for you.

Material	Prediction	Result
Metal spoon	✓	✓✓

Parts of a simple series circuit

Modelling circuits

1 You are going to make a model of a circuit. Stand in a circle with your hands by your side. Your teacher will tell you which component you are.

- If you are a wire, stand with your arms stretched out wide and wiggle them.

- If you are a battery, jump up and down to show how much energy you have.

- If you are bulb, sway from side to side.

- If you are a buzzer, say 'Buzzzzzzz!'

- If you are a switch, decide whether you are a closed or open switch.

  - Closed switch: stand with your arms stretched out wide. Shout 'closed' and everything will work. The buzzer will buzz and the bulb will light up.

  - Open switch: stand with one arm stretched out wide and the other arm by your side. Shout 'open' and everything will stop working.

2 Now join hands to make a circuit. If everyone is joined together, everything will work.

3 Draw your closed circuit, showing the components.

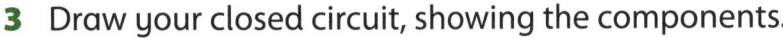

Components

 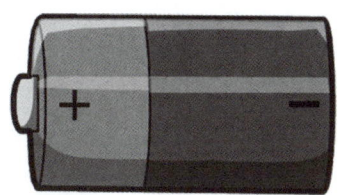 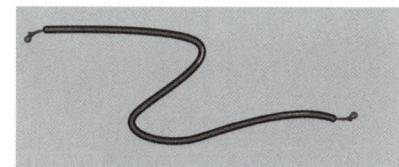

Label each component in the pictures. Use the words from the box.

battery   bulb   wire

Stretch zone

Research how a filament bulb works.

a Draw a picture to show your ideas.

b What problems could occur if components overheat when electricity passes through them?

More electrical components

Electric music

1 Set up a circuit that contains the components shown below.

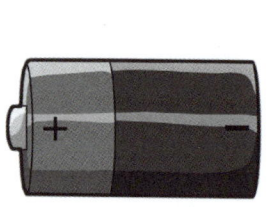  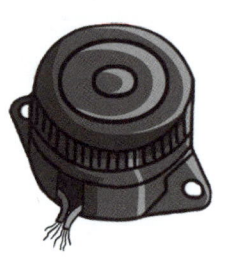

You will need:
components to make a circuit, a type of buzzer or bell.

2 Close the switch and test if you can hear your buzzer or bell.

> **Stretch zone**
>
> If you can't hear the buzzer, make a list of the checks you should make.
>
> Check 1: _____
>
> Check 2: _____
>
> Check 3: _____
>
> Change any faulty components for new ones and check the circuit once again.

3 Practise closing and opening the switch to make music.

4 Work with other teams with different sounds to make up a tune by opening and closing the switches.

5 Perform your music.

Make a game

1 List all the components that you predict are being
used in this game in the space below.

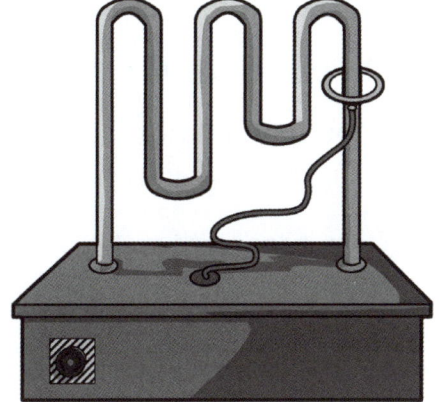

2 Explain how the circuit is being used.

You can use these questions to help you:

- Where will the electricity come from? Battery or mains?

- How will the battery be connected to the other components?

- Why does the buzzer sound? What happens to the circuit?

- Could you connect a bulb to this circuit?

- Where would the bulb be connected in the circuit?

Sketch out the components and how they link together in the box below.

Open and close switches

Look at the diagrams of circuits.

Will the bulb light up or not?

- If you predict that the bulb will light up, draw a tick ✓ in the diagram box.

- If you predict that the bulb will not light up, draw a cross ✗ in the diagram box.

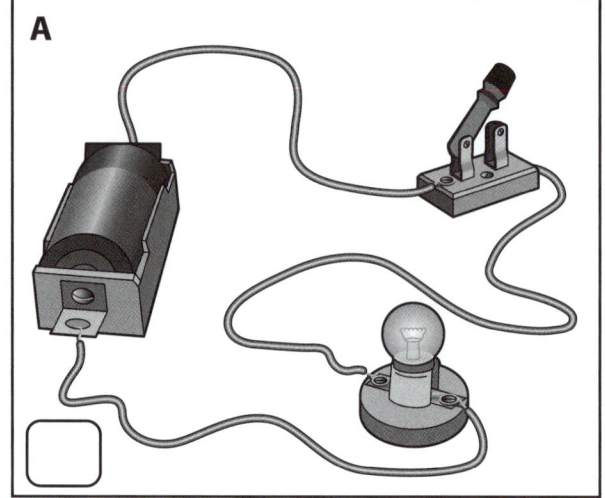

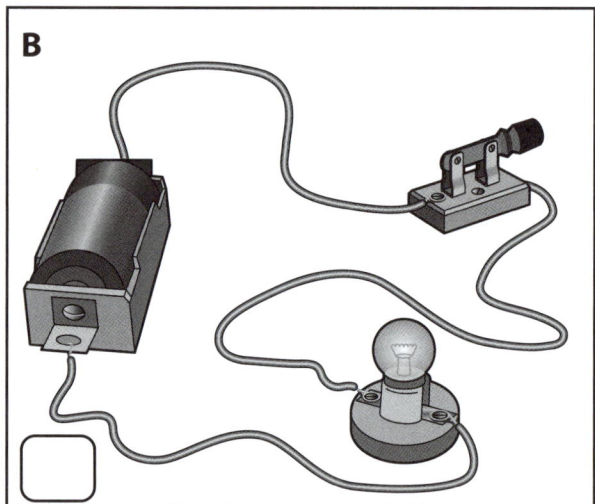

 **Stretch zone**

Explain why you made the predictions.

Scientists test their predictions. How can you test yours?

Circuits

1   Look at the diagrams of circuits. Predict what will happen to the bulbs in each circuit.

A   **B**

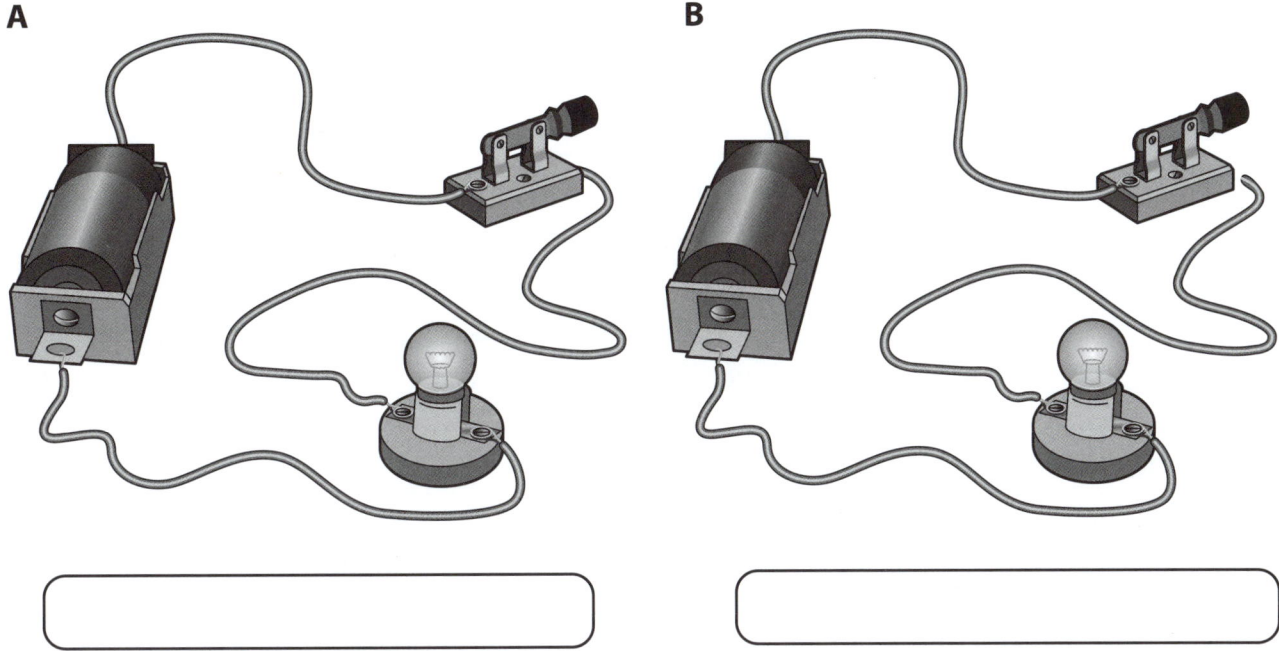

2   Which label below matches circuit **A**? Write the correct label in the box below
    the diagram.

3   Which label below matches circuit **B**? Write the correct label in the box below
    the diagram.

Labels:
The bulb will not light up. The bulb will light up brightly. The bulb will light up but not very brightly.

Scientists always check their investigations. If you have time, build the circuits more than once to check your results.

4   Check your answers by building the circuits with your partner.

    Were your predictions correct?   **yes**   **no**

Making circuits with switches

Exploring circuits

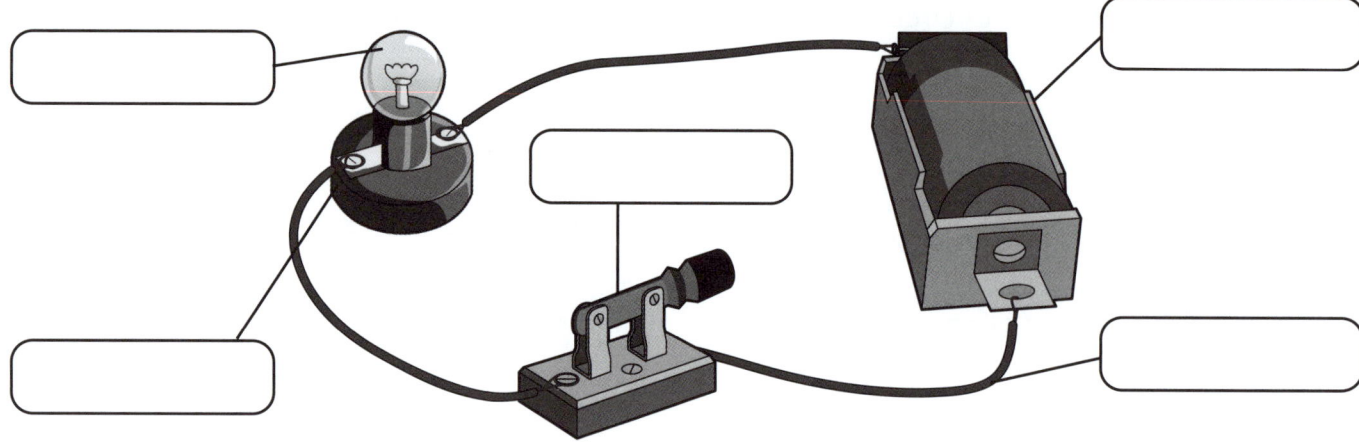

 **1** Label the circuit. Use the words from the box below.

> battery   bulb   connector   switch   wire

2 Look at the diagram of the circuit. Which component do you need to move to make the bulb go out? _____

Stretch zone

Predict what will make the bulb glow less brightly.

_____

_____

Drawing circuits

 1 Draw a line from the picture of each component to its name. One has been done for you.

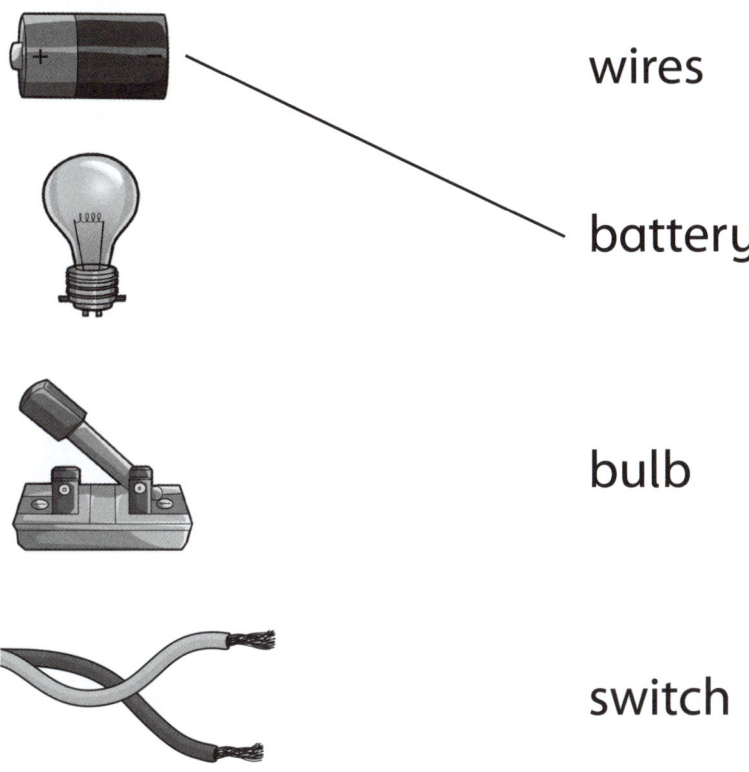

wires

battery

bulb

switch

2 Research three other components that can be added to an electrical circuit. Draw an example of each and write down what it is used for.

Electrical current flows

Designing circuits

Work with a partner or small team for this activity.

1   In the space below, design one circuit that will work and one that will not work.

2   Show your designs to another team and ask them to predict whether or not the circuits will work.

Tick ✓ the circuit design if they predict it will work. Draw a cross ✗ if they predict it will not.

3   They should then test their predictions by building the circuits.

   a   Did the circuits work as you designed them to?
   Circle the answer.   **yes**   **no**

   b   Did the other team predict correctly?
   Circle the answer.   **yes**   **no**

Designing more circuits

1 Build a simple circuit using wires, a bulb and a battery.

2 Leave a gap in the circuit to connect your switch.

3 Push a paper fastener through the loop of a paperclip.

4 Push the paper fastener through your piece of card to hold the paperclip in place.

You will need:
components to make a circuit, two paper fasteners, a paperclip, a piece of card.

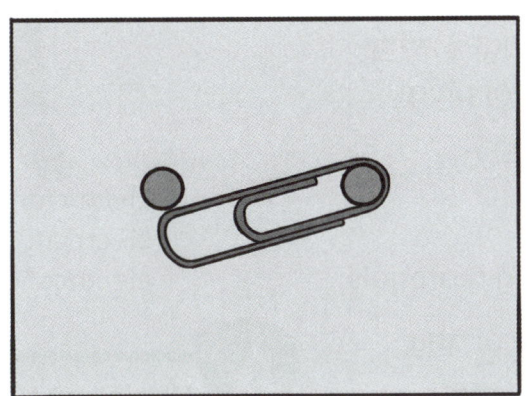

5 Push the other paper fastener through the cardboard.

Check that when the paperclip is moved it can touch this paper fastener.

6 Why does the paperclip have to touch both of the paper fasteners? Cross out the wrong answer.

To complete the circuit.   **To break the circuit.**

7 Connect the loose wires to each of the paper fasteners underneath the cardboard.

Close the switch.

8 What happens to the bulb? Cross out the wrong answer.

The bulb lights.   **The bulb does not light.**

Stretch zone ➡

Could you use this binder clip to make a switch?

Design a circuit to test this.

Conductors and insulators

Why are insulators important?

Electricians and electrical engineers work with electrical circuits. They always turn the electricity off to make it safe. However, some people are not so sensible. They may forget or may not be able to do this.

We are protected from electrical shocks by insulating materials such as plastics. That is why we should only touch the plastic parts of plugs or wires.

Electricians always turn off the electricity before working on electrical circuits

 You are going to survey some insulating materials.

1 Look around the room. Make a note of any electrical insulating materials being used.

 **Warning!** Never put anything metal into a socket.

2 Complete the table to record five examples.

Location of insulator	Material it is made from	How is it being used?

3 Design and make a small poster to place near a socket or electrical device. Your poster should:

- warn people of the dangers of electricity
- explain why insulators are so important.

Which material is the best for a screwdriver handle?

Let's investigate which material is the best material to use for the handle of a screwdriver that an electrician would use.

1 Should you be looking for an insulating material or a conducting material for a screwdriver handle? Why?

2 Use the circuit you used earlier to test if materials are good conductors.

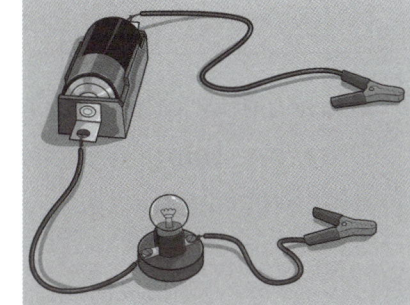

Remember: If the bulb lights up, then electricity must be moving through the material from the battery to the bulb.

3 Use the table below to record your results. An example has been added for you.

Material	Good conductor	Poor conductor
paper		✓

4 Group the materials into good conductors and poor conductors.

5 Should your insulating material be a good conductor or a poor conductor?

6 What other properties of the material will you use to decide the best material for the handle?

Warning! Do not touch any bare wires. Keep the battery in the battery holder. Discuss why this is important.

7 Present your ideas and findings.

Dangers of electricity

Electrical safety

 1 Complete the safety instructions. Use the words in the box.

broken	burn	socket	wet

> ⚠ **Keep safe when you use electricity!**
>
> Never touch _____ wires.
>
> Do not touch sockets with _____ hands.
>
> Electric shocks can _____ our skin.
>
> Never put things into an electrical _____.

2 Draw a floor plan of your house. Draw one thing in each room that uses electricity.

3 Think of one safety rule to remember when you use each electrical appliance you have drawn.

Danger!

1 Look at the symbols.

What are they all telling you?

2 Design your own electricity danger symbol in the box.

3 Draw your symbol on five sticky notes.

Look around the room. Put the safety symbols where you think they are most needed.

Warning! Do not touch any electrical appliances, sockets or wires.

What I have learned about electricity

What went well

1 Think about what you have learned.

2 Talk to a friend about something that went well in this unit.

3 Tick ✓ the boxes to rate yourself.

I can identify common appliances that run on electricity.	That's easy. ☐ That's challenging. ☐	Pages 96–99
I can make a simple electrical circuit and recognise its basic parts.	That's easy. ☐ That's challenging. ☐	Pages 100–105
I can identify whether or not a lamp will light in a simple series circuit.	That's easy. ☐ That's challenging. ☐	Pages 106–109
I recognise some common conductors and insulators.	That's easy. ☐ That's challenging. ☐	Pages 110–111
I know the dangers of electricity.	That's easy. ☐ That's challenging. ☐	Pages 112–113

 If you want to know more or need to check, go back to the pages in your Student Book.

Investigate like a scientist

Making fairy lights

You are going to make a string of 10 fairy lights.

1 Make sure all of your bulbs work before you start the construction of the string of fairy lights.

2 Connect the bulbs and batteries together using wires and connectors.

3 How many batteries will you need to make sure all of the bulbs shine brightly?

_____

4 Predict what would happen if one of the bulbs stopped working.

_____

5 Explain why it would not be a good idea to wire all of the lights in your school in this way.

_____

Key words

 Look carefully at the key words and make a word wall.

decibel | loud | pattern | pitch | quiet | sound | travel | vibrate | volume

1 Write each word on a piece of card. Make the writing large and clear.

2 If you know what the word means, write the meaning on the back of the card.
   If you do not know the meaning, leave the back of the card blank.

3 Place your word cards onto a wall so they look like the bricks of a wall.

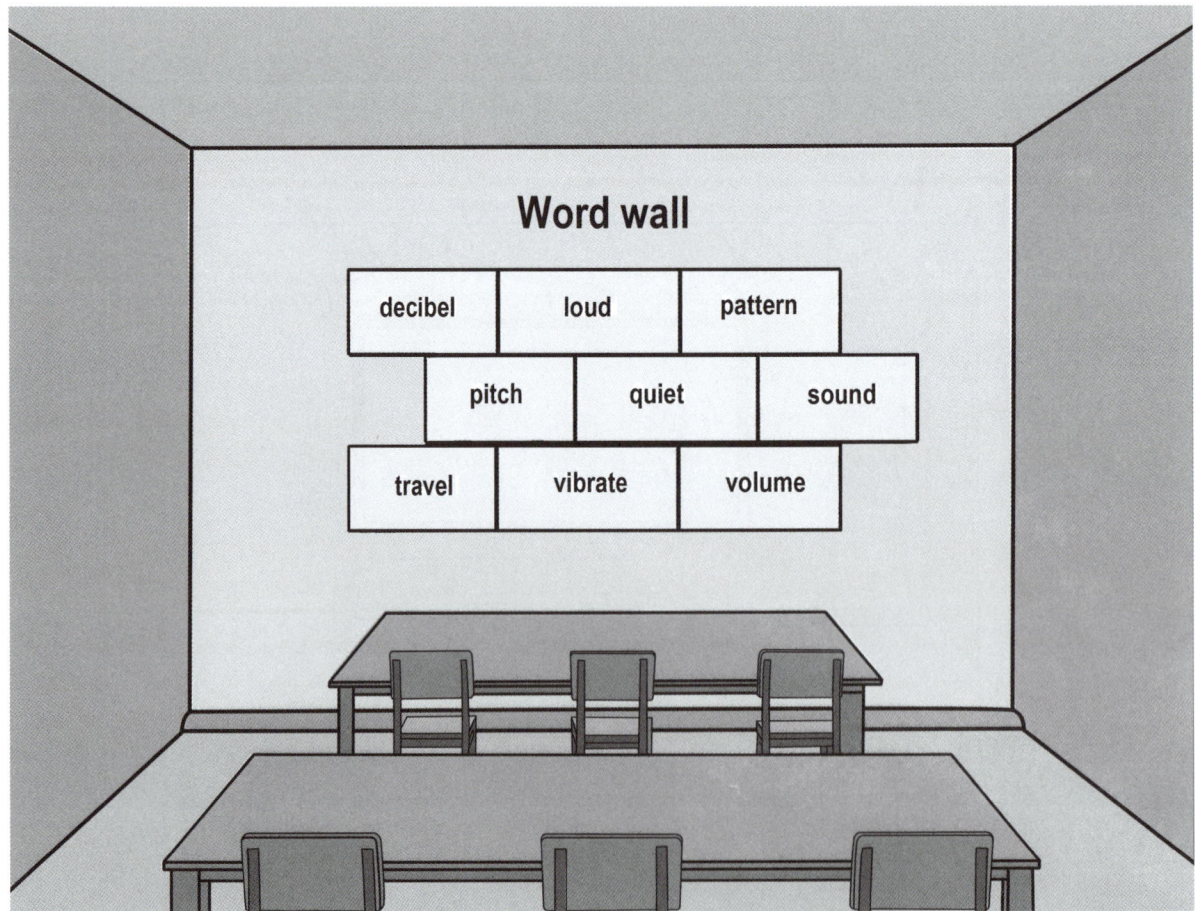

4 When you learn the meaning of a key word, write it down on the back of the card and
   place it back on your wall.

Introduction

What I would like to learn

 Look at pages 116–117 of your Student Book. Think about what you might be learning in this unit.

- Read the information and look at the photographs.

- Find out what the science facts are.

- Does any of the information look familiar?

1 List three things about sound that you would like to know more about.

1 _____

2 _____

3 _____

 **2** Read the key words below.

> decibel   loud   pattern   pitch   quiet   sound   travel   vibrate   volume

Have you seen any of the words before? Do you understand them?

3 Sort and write each of the key words into one of the boxes below.

I understand these words.

I need to find out what these words mean.

How sounds are made

Vibrations and sounds

 We need vibrations to hear sounds. This activity supports the investigation on page 118 of your Student Book.

1 Hold a 30-cm ruler on the edge of your desk with one hand. Place it so that 15 cm overhangs the edge.

2 With your other hand, pull the end of the ruler down and let it go.

What happens to the end of the ruler?

3 What happens when the ruler stops vibrating?

4 Investigate what happens when you change the length of the ruler that overhangs the desk. Use an overhang of 5 cm, 10 cm, 20 cm and 25 cm.

5 Record your findings in the table below. Does the sound get higher or lower in pitch compared to the 15-cm overhang? Tick ✓ the correct column.

Length of overhang (cm)	The pitch gets higher	The pitch gets lower
5		
10		
20		
25		

 6 What have you learned about the length of the overhang and the sounds and vibrations produced?

1   Make a small drum using a large bowl.

Stretch a piece of cling film over the bowl and fix it in place with sticky tape. Make sure the cling film is very tight.

2   Hit the drum with a stick or your hand. Observe what happens.

3   Put a handful of dry rice onto the cling film and then hit the drum.

   a   What happens to the rice?

   b   What causes this? Use the internet or books to find out more.

Observing and measuring sound

Compose a tune

Show someone the guitar you made, following the instructions on page 119 of your Student Book. Demonstrate how to play your guitar.

 Explain how you can change the sound of the guitar.

Describe the vibrations that the strings make.

 You are going to compose a tune on your guitar.

1   Play notes by changing the length of the strings using your fingers. Then pluck the strings.

2   Practise making loud and quiet (soft) sounds by changing how hard you pluck the strings.

3   Let someone else play your guitar.

4   Form a band with other people. You can use objects around the room.

   • Try using pots and pans as drums.

   • Try using pencils and desk legs as percussion instruments.

Display information about sound

Remember that we measure sound in decibels (dB).

Look carefully at the table of results, which shows the sound level of a variety of sounds.

You are going to draw a bar chart to present the results shown in the table.

Type of sound	Sound level (dB)
rustling leaves	10
whisper	20
conversation	60
busy traffic	70
vacuum cleaner	80
music through headphones	100
a child screaming	110
causes humans pain	130
jet taking off	140
permanent damage to the ear	160

Think about:

How big does the bar chart need to be?

Which is the horizontal axis and which is the vertical axis?

What information will you plot on each axis?

Your scale:

- What number will you need to start with?

- What is the highest number you will need?

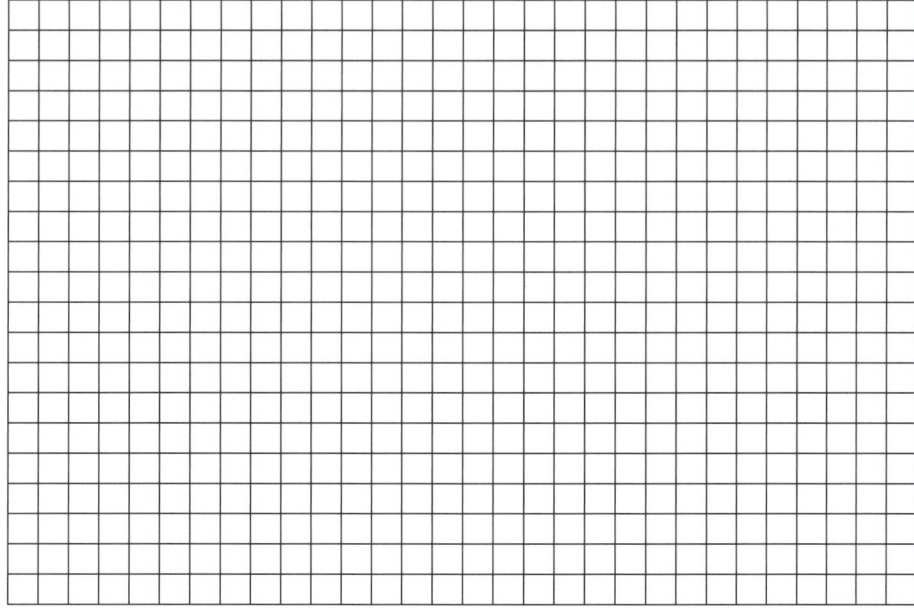

Warning! Use a pencil and a ruler to draw and plot your bar chart. This will make it neater and much easier to read.

How does sound travel to our ears?

Sounds in the home

Which are the quietest and the noisiest rooms at home?

1   Make predictions.

    a   Predict which room will be the quietest. _____

    b   Predict which room will be the noisiest. _____

2   Walk around your home listening all of the time.

3   Find the quietest room in your home.

    Write the name of the room. _____

 4   What makes this room quiet?

5   Now find the noisiest room in your home.

    Write the name of the room. _____

 6   **a**   What makes this room noisy?

    b   What could you do to the room to make it less noisy?

7   Write your ideas for how to soundproof the noisy room.

Use your hearing to identify materials

Can you identify materials with your hearing?

Work with a partner for this investigation.

1 The first person sits down and closes their eyes.

2 The second person hits a material with a pencil to make a sound.

3 The first person guesses what the material is. They must give a reason why they think it is this material.

4 Record the first person's guesses in the table.

Tick ✓ the box each time the person's guess is correct.

First person:

Guessed material	Was the guess correct?

5 Mix up the materials and swap roles.

Record the second person's guesses in the table.

Tick ✓ the box each time the person's guess is correct.

Second person:

Guessed material	Was the guess correct?

Investigating how sound travels

Making sounds appear louder

Warning! Never let anybody shout near your ears. Loud sounds can damage your hearing.

You can design and make a device to help you hear sounds. These are called hearing aids.

In a later activity, you will make a device called a hearing trumpet. In this activity, you are going to make some giant ears!

The larger ear shapes collect the sound vibrations in the air and help them to pass into your ear.

1 Draw your own design for some giant ears.
Make and test your device.

2 Demonstrate your device to someone else.
What is one way you could improve your design?

How does water change the way we hear sound?

This activity supports the investigation on page 125 of your Student Book.

1   Gently blow over the neck of an empty bottle. Can you make a sound?

2   What made the sound in the bottle?

3   Add some water to your bottle and gently blow over the neck like you did before.

4   What happens to the sound now?

5   Add different amounts of water and investigate the sounds you make.

6   Is there a pattern?

7   What do you conclude from your investigation? Circle the best answer to finish these sentences.

   a   When I added more water the volume of the sound

   got louder.   got quieter.   stayed the same.

   b   When I added water the sound got

   higher.   lower.

How can we make sounds louder?

Does distance make sounds fainter?

This activity supports the investigation on page 126 of your Student Book.

Can you make a tuning fork sound louder?

> Some people say a sound gets fainter and others say it gets quieter. These are the same thing.

1 Hit the fork on a hard surface and hold it in the air. Listen to the sound it makes.

What do you hear? _____

2 Walk five metres away from the tuning fork and record your observations. Repeat your observations every five metres until you are 20 metres away.

3 Record your observations in the table below. Circle the correct answer.

Distance from tuning fork (m)	Observation
5	the sound was *fainter / louder* than next to the tuning fork
10	the sound was *fainter / louder* than next to the tuning fork
15	the sound was *fainter / louder* than next to the tuning fork
20	the sound was *fainter / louder* than next to the tuning fork

4 Complete the conclusion by circling the correct answer.

What happens to the sound when you move further away from the tuning fork?

It becomes louder.   It becomes fainter.

Your string telephone

This activity supports the investigation on page 127.

You are going to make a string telephone.

You will need: two paper cups, a piece of string.

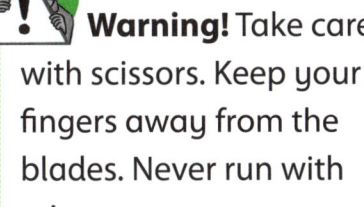

Warning! Take care with scissors. Keep your fingers away from the blades. Never run with scissors.

1 Take two cups.

2 Use scissors to make a small hole in the bottom of each cup.

3 Push one end of the string through one of the holes and fix it into place by tying a knot. Then push the other end of the string through the hole in the other cup and tie this in place.

4 Hold one of the cups to your ear and ask a partner to hold the other cup to their ear. Move back slowly so the string is tight.

5 Talk to each other through your telephone.

6 In the box below draw a diagram to show how sound travels from your mouth to your partner's ear when using your phone.

Some materials stop sound travelling

Protecting your ears

This activity supports the investigation on pages 128–129 of your Student Book.

1 a Think about which workers need to use ear defenders.

b List as many jobs as you can where the workers need to protect their ears.

_____   _____

_____   _____

_____   _____

2 Design and make your own ear defenders.
First make a plan.

a List some materials that will reduce the sound reaching your ears.

_____   _____   _____

_____   _____   _____

_____   _____   _____

b The outer case should be made of a hard material. What materials could you use for this?

_____

c Draw your design. Label the materials you have chosen and show how you will keep the ear defenders on your head.

3 Make your ear defenders.

4 Test them to find out if they protect your ears from sound.

Survey of uses of sound insulation

1 Walk around your school or home.
   Observe how sound insulators are used.

2 Record your findings in the table below. One has been done for you.

Place seen	Materials used	How is it being used
window	fabric curtains	to reduce the traffic noise

3 Describe what school or home would be like if there were no sound-proofing materials.
   What problems would you have?

Investigating wave patterns of sound

How can we change the pitch of a sound?

Make a test instrument.

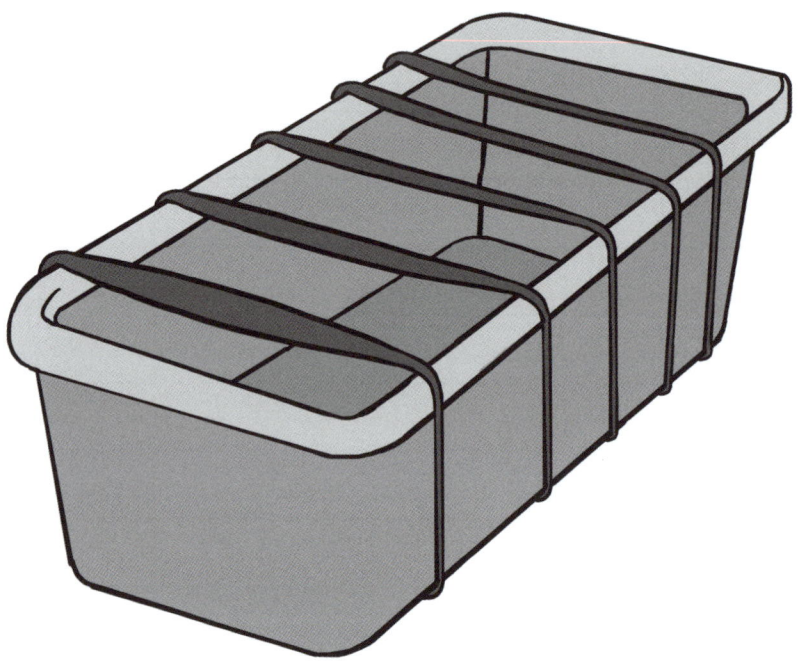

1. Place five or six elastic bands of differing widths around an empty plastic or cardboard box. The box helps to amplify or increase the volume of the sound. The box itself vibrates and also the air inside it is made to vibrate.

2. Pluck each string in turn.

   What happens to the sound? Circle the correct answer.

   The thicker the band the **higher / lower** the pitch.

   The thinner the band the **higher / lower** the pitch.

3. The faster a band or string vibrates, the higher the pitch of sound produced.

   Which band vibrated the fastest? _____

 **Stretch zone**

Plan an investigation to find out what happens when the length of the elastic band gets shorter. Use the internet or books to find out more about the length of strings and the pitch of sound.

Oscilloscopes

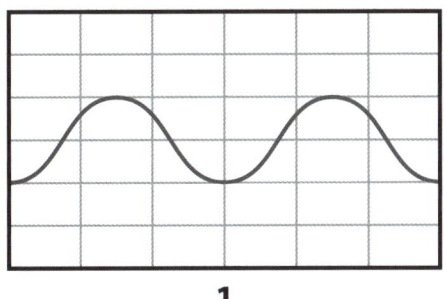

1

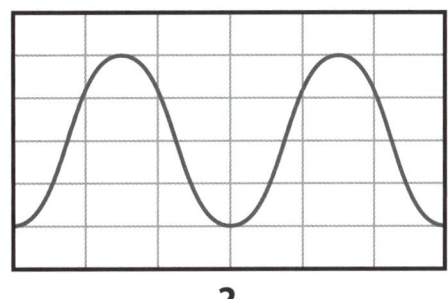

2

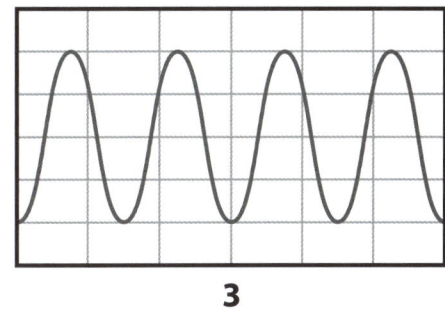

3

Match the diagrams of oscilloscope displays to the descriptions below.

Each description may match more than one wave pattern. Write the number(s) of the correct diagram(s) next to each description.

A   There are only two waves. These waves are made by low-pitched sounds.

_____

B   There are four waves. These waves are made by high-pitched sounds.

_____

C   These waves are high – they are made by loud sounds.

_____

D   These waves are not very high – they are made by quieter sounds.

_____

Remember: The number of waves tells us the pitch of a sound.
The height of the waves tells us how loud a sound is.

Investigating the volume of sounds

We all hear sounds differently

 Do different people hear differently?

1 Listen to the sound that your teacher makes.

On a piece of paper, write whether it is loud or soft.

Write whether it is high or low pitched.

2 Show your answers to the rest of the class when your teacher tells you to.

3 Listen to other sounds that your teacher plays.

Write whether each one is loud or soft and high or low pitched.

4 Show your answers to the rest of the class when your teacher tells you to.

 **5 a** Did everyone get the same results? Discuss why.

b What does this tell us about the way we hear things?

c Write your conclusion below.

_____

_____

_____

_____

Super hearing at home

Amaze people at home by showing them how good your hearing is.

This activity supports the investigation on page 133 of your Student Book.

You are going to make an ear cone.

This activity supports the investigation on page 133 of your Student Book.

You will need: a large piece of paper (the bigger the piece of paper the bigger and better the ear cone will be), sticky tape or glue.

1   Roll the paper to make an ear cone like the one in the picture.

2   Ask someone to help you put the sticky tape on the cone to hold it in place.

3   Tell them to keep the ear cone a secret!

4   Ask other people at home to whisper some words while you are in the next room. Don't tell them you have an ear cone.

5   Go into the next room and listen using your ear cone. You should be able to hear the whispers!

6   Show the other people at home how to use the ear cone.

    The person using the ear cone will be able to hear sounds that the others cannot hear.

7   Explain how the ear cone helps us to hear quiet sounds.

Making music

Making music with bottles

 This activity supports the investigation on page 135 of your Student Book.

You are going to show your family how to make music using glass bottles and water.

There are two different methods. You can try both methods or choose one.

You will need: five or six glass bottles of roughly the same size, a wooden spoon or pencil.

Warning! Be careful with glass, it is very sharp when broken.

1   Use clean, empty glass bottles.

2   Pour different amounts of water into each bottle.

3   Using either method 1 or 2, put the bottles in order so that the pitch of the sound gets higher and higher.

Method 1

Using the wooden spoon or pencil, gently tap each bottle and listen to the sound.

Method 2

Hold each bottle and gently blow over the top of the bottle to make a sound.

4   Try to play your favourite tune using the bottles.

5   Now try making a bigger band or orchestra.

Ask other people to join in.

- Use the glass bottles.

- Also use the guitar you made on page 119 of your Student Book and the pots and pans you used earlier.

- Try using other objects around the house to make music. Make sure you ask permission first.

Making music with glasses

1 Run your finger around the rim of a glass. The vibration from your finger goes into the air in the glass and makes a sound.

Warning! Be very careful with glass. Do not press onto it too hard. Never pick up broken glass with your hands. Why do you think this is so important?

2 What do you think will happen to the pitch if you pour some water into the glasses?

3 Set up six glasses and add different amounts of water to each.

4 Try to make a tune.

5 Complete the paragraph below by filling in the gaps.

Use words from the box. You can use some more than once.

> air   finger   higher   pitch   sound   vibrations

The glass made a sound because _____ from my _____

make _____ waves in the air. These _____ waves travel to

my ears and I can hear the sound. As water is added there is less _____ in

the glass to vibrate so the _____ of the sound is _____ .

What I have learned about sounds

 What went well

1 Think about what you have learned.

2 Talk to a friend about something that went well in this unit.

3 Tick ✓ the boxes to rate yourself.

I know how *sounds are made* when *objects, materials or air vibrate*.	That's easy. ☐ That's challenging. ☐	Pages 118–121
I know how *sound travels through different* materials.	That's easy. ☐ That's challenging. ☐	Pages 122–127
I know how *some materials stop sound* travelling.	That's easy. ☐ That's challenging. ☐	Pages 128–129
I know that *pitch describes* how high or low a sound is.	That's easy. ☐ That's challenging. ☐	Pages 130–133
I know how *to use musical instruments to* change pitch.	That's easy. ☐ That's challenging. ☐	Pages 134–135

 If you want to know more or need to check, go back to the pages in your Student Book.

Investigate like a scientist

Investigating string telephones

1 Make a string telephone like the one opposite. Use five metres of string.

2 Hold one cup to your ear. Ask your partner to speak softly into the other cup.

   Move five metres apart so the string is tight.

3 How well can you hear your partner from five metres away, when they are whispering into the telephone?

_____

4 How well can you hear your partner whispering from five metres away without the telephone?

_____

5 Plan and carry out your investigation. Some of the factors you could investigate are as follows.

   - Does the length of string affect the telephone?

   - Does the tightness of the string affect the telephone?

   - Do different types and thicknesses of string affect the telephone?

   - Do different materials for the cups affect the telephone?

   - Do different sizes of cups affect the telephone?

6 Present your ideas and findings.

Quiz Yourself

These quiz questions and activities are intended to encourage students to reflect on their learning and to reinforce their developing knowledge about scientific concepts in a fun way. They are flexible enough to be individual, pair or group activities. The questions can be used in a number of ways.

- Questions can be selected from this section to supplement work carried out during each module, to act as extra tasks and support for individuals, groups and whole classes. In this way, they can aid differentiation.
- Students can tackle the relevant questions at the end of each module to review learning and supplement the 'What I have learned' sections.
- Students can undertake questions at the end of a series of modules or even at the end of the year to review learning. The questions could be set in batches over a series of lessons or even taken as a small timed test – although this is not their main purpose.

1 Solids, Liquids and Gases

1 **a** Which container would you use for a liquid, a solid and a gas? Label the containers to show your answers.

b Draw the particles for each state of matter in or on the containers.

2 Read the four different changes of state.

Write the state of matter at the start and the end. One has been done for you.

a Melting a candle

solid ⟶ _liquid_

b Boiling water

⟶

c Melting chocolate

⟶

d Freezing water to make ice cubes

⟶

3 a Complete the table. Write in the properties of solids, liquids and gases.

Property	Solid	Liquid	Gas
How dense is it?			
How easy is it to squash (compress)?			
Does it flow?			
Does it have a fixed shape?			
Does it have a fixed volume?			

b Label the particle diagrams as either solid, liquid or gas.

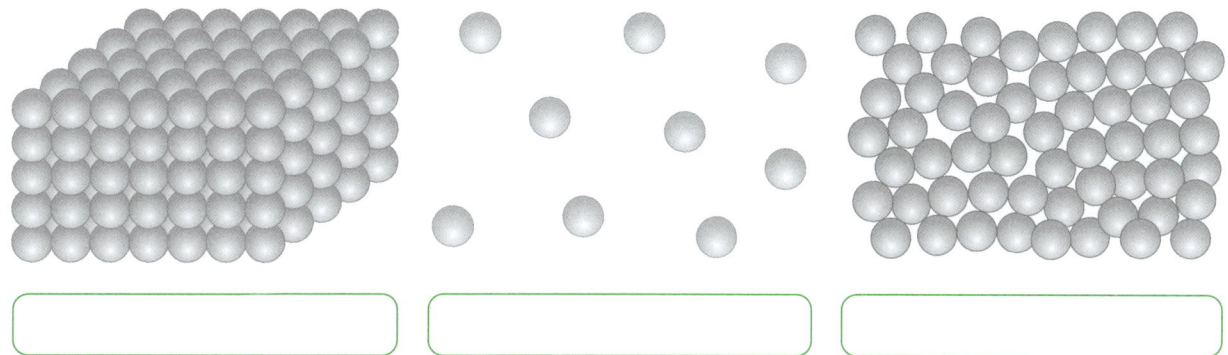

② Habitats

4 Look at the pieces of equipment. We can use them to capture or count animals and plants in their habitats. Draw a line from each plant or insect to the best piece of equipment.

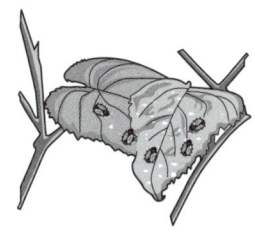  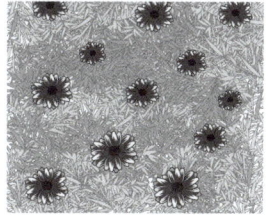

 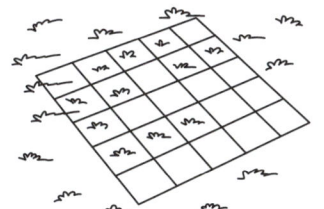 

5 Follow the curly lines to find each animal's habitat.

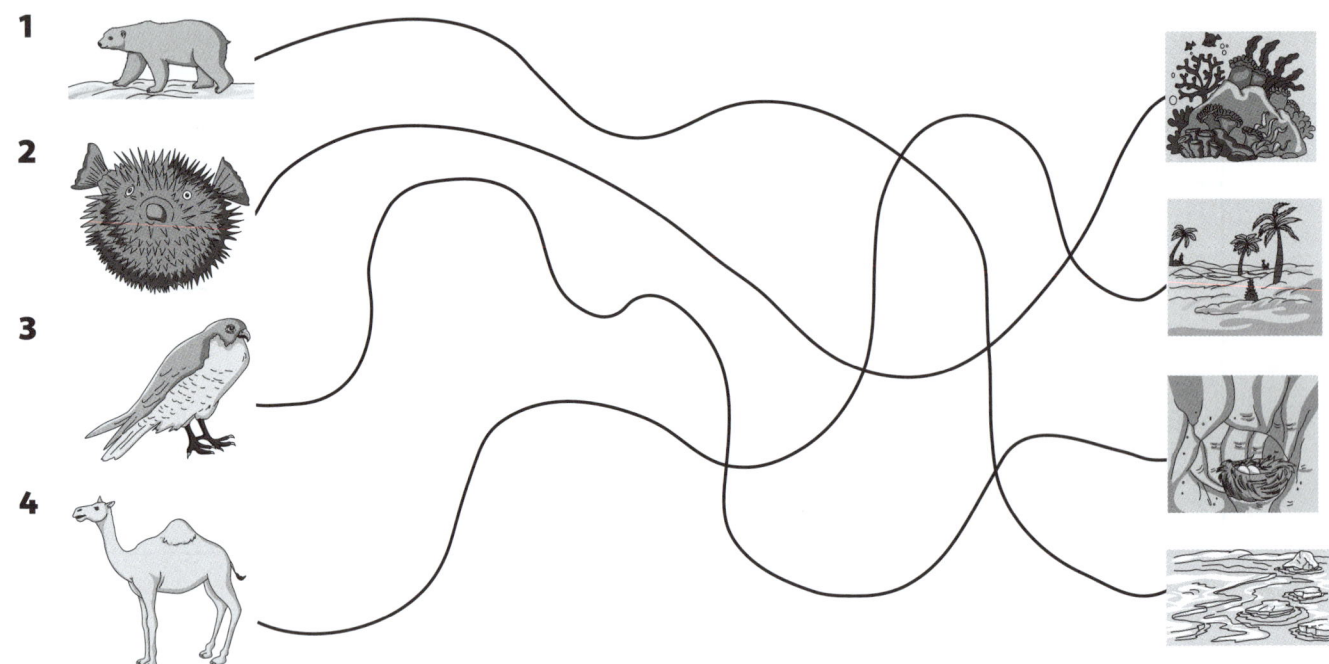

3 Digestion and Food Chains

6 Label the diagram below. Use the words in the box.

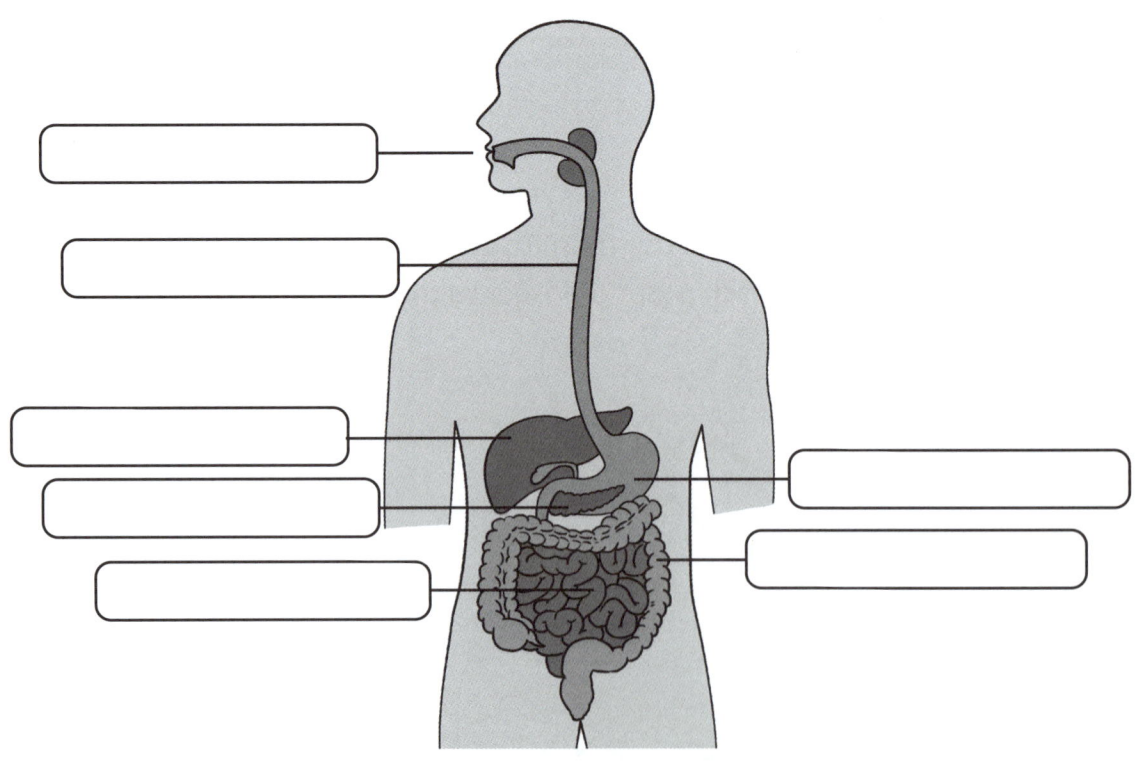

large intestine   liver   mouth   oesophagus
pancreas   small intestine   stomach

7 Draw arrows on the diagram to make a food web. Remember to draw each arrow in the direction of the flow of energy.

- Colour the producers green.

- Colour the primary consumers (herbivores) brown.

- Colour the secondary and tertiary consumers (carnivores) red.

4 Electricity

8 a Look at the pictures of some components of electrical circuits. Tick ✓ each one you need to make a test circuit.

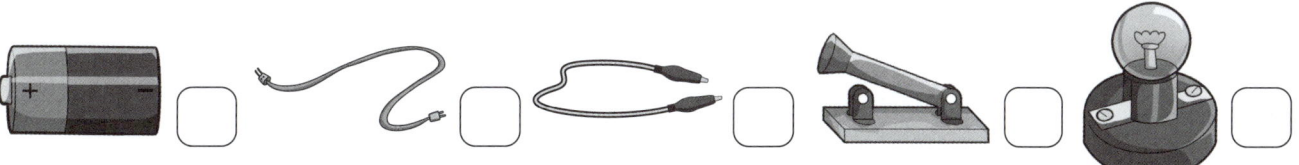

b Use the components you have chosen to draw a test circuit that will work.

9 Read the definitions. Circle the correct word for each definition. Highlight the bold letter of each correct answer. What word do these letters make?

- This component makes electrical energy for a circuit.

  a wire   **b** battery   **c** switch   **d** lamp

- This component makes a loud noise.

  s connector   **t** switch   **u** buzzer   **v** lamp

- This connects the components in a circuit.

  l connector   **m** battery   **n** lamp   **o** buzzer

- This component is used to complete or break a circuit.

  a connector   **b** switch   **c** buzzer   **d** lamp

The letters I have highlighted make this word: _____

5 Sounds

10 a Find the following words about sound in the wordsearch. Circle each word in the grid when you find it.

> amplify   decibel   guitar   loud   material   pitch   quiet   travel
> tuning fork   vibrate   volume

t	a	m	p	l	i	f	y	p	y
e	u	l	n	q	u	m	b	i	d
d	w	n	v	i	b	r	a	t	e
s	q	u	i	e	t	k	f	c	c
v	p	g	o	n	a	c	p	h	i
o	g	z	u	t	g	j	r	a	b
l	o	u	d	i	v	f	i	h	e
u	a	v	g	s	t	c	o	q	l
m	a	t	e	r	i	a	l	r	z
e	t	r	a	v	e	l	r	x	k

b Write a definition for each of the following words:

volume: _____

_____

pitch: _____

_____

decibel: _____

_____

11 The table shows data about sound levels.

Type of sound	Sound level (dB)
rustling leaves	10
whisper	20
conversation	60
busy traffic	70
vacuum cleaner	80
music through headphones	100
a child screaming	110
causes humans pain	130
jet taking off	140
permanent damage to the ear	160

a Draw a chart or graph to present the data in the table.

b Use the table and your chart or graph to answer these questions.

What is the sound level of a whisper? _____

What is the loudest sound? _____